Outdoorsman's FIX-IT Book

An Outdoor Life Book

Outdoorsman's
FIX-IT Book

Monte Burch

Drawings by
Frank Schwarz

OUTDOOR LIFE

HARPER & ROW

NEW YORK • LONDON

Designed by Jeff Fitschen

Manufactured in the United States of America

Contents

The rollers • The tie-downs • Camper trailers • Checking the gas system

Acknowledgments

The author wishes to thank the following firms for their assistance in supplying photographs for this book:

Slaymaker Lock Company
Luger Industries
Thermos
Dutton-Lainson Company
Tempo Products Company
Valspar Corporation
Shaler Company
LPS Research Laboratories, Inc.
Hooker Chemical Corporation
Champion Spark Plug Company
Farber Brothers, Inc.
McCulloh Corporation
Mirro Corporation
Bernz-O-Matic Corporation

Outdoorsman's
FIX-IT Book

Introduction

A few generations ago, taking to the woods meant carrying a blanket roll, frying pan, a sack of flour, salt and a slab of cured pork side. Not so today; the sophisticated outdoorsman, including auto campers, hunters, fishermen and even bird watchers, takes to the field with an array of equipment that would astound even an old-time "traveling tinkerer." Naturally the more equipment, the more time and money it requires to keep it working properly. And keeping equipment in good working condition is a necessity, not only for your own personal comfort and safety, but for the safety of the fragile environment you're visiting. It is every outdoorsman's responsibility to see that his outboard motor, chain saw, or whatever, is working properly and not spewing out avoidable clouds of oil and smoke.

Unfortunately we have become a "throw-away" world. If something doesn't work, we merely pitch it onto the garbage heap along with millions of other items just like it. This was not the case with the great and rugged people who founded and developed our country; our fathers and grandfathers, who were so strongly tied to the outdoor life. The most important items on a farm or ranch years ago were a coil of baling wire and a pair of pliers. Almost anything could be repaired with this pair, from split tire rims to splints for broken bones. We need to preserve this rugged outdoor reliance. If a sleeping bag becomes torn, or a tent becomes a little ragged, fix it up, patch it, put on a good coat of waterproofing. Don't throw it away just because the guy in the next campsite has a newer, more brilliantly colored tent.

When the outdoorsman starts to care for and repair his own equipment, he establishes in himself that same old self-reliance that has made our country so great. In many cases, knowing how to repair your equipment while in the bush is an absolute necessity, and may well mean your life. This is particularly true for outdoorsmen using snowmobiles or outboards. If a stubborn outboard won't start and a bad storm is brewing, the knowledgeable outdoorsman who can search for the trouble, find it and fix it, is the one who will be back on the lake the next day. By the same token, a snowmobile can get an outdoorsman so far back into the bush, and so fast, that he absolutely needs to know all he can about how to care for and repair any equipment he will need to rely on for survival.

1 Axes, Knives and Saws

If I could only take one item with me into the woods, it would be a good axe. With this tool, I could survive for as long as I had water and a natural food supply. The steel head could be used to strike against flint for producing fire. The axe could naturally be used to chop down trees for fire, shelter and animal traps, and to make primitive spears and weapons. A full-size axe could even be a formidable weapon, if need be. If sharp enough, it could be used to skin and dress out anything from squirrel to moose. There comes my second choice; a good whetstone would make the axe even more valuable, and is basically the only piece of equipment needed to keep an axe working. If the axe handle breaks or you loose a wedge, you can manufacture either using just the metal head.

A good axe or hatchet is essential to any outdoorsman. If you're a backpacker, it will probably be an ultralight belt hatchet. If you prefer to car camp or saddle pack, it will be a good axe. Many big-game hunters prefer a combination light hatchet and belt knife combined with a small whetstone in one sheath; an ideal combination for dressing out big game such as elk.

AXES

In choosing an axe or hatchet, pick a good-quality one; a cheap axe will cause you to repay its price many times over. Many surplus and drugstore axes are made of untempered steel and the first time you try to cut a hardwood log you'll end up with an axe that won't even cut matchsticks. The edge will roll over and in many cases simply chip and dent. However, a good axe will require very little maintenance. The main thing is that the blade must be kept honed as sharp as possible and at it's proper cutting angle or you run the risk of serious

3

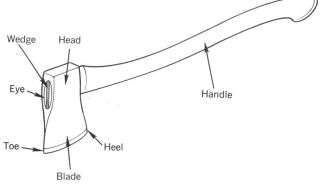

The parts of an axe.

injury from a glancing blow. A woodsman's life literally depends on his axe blade when he's alone in the bush and far from civilization. A bad gash on the leg, and no other means of transportation, means he could die. You can also work yourself to death trying to cut with a dull axe blade, or any other tool for that matter. So keeping axes and knives absolutely razor sharp is one job no experienced woodsman neglects. Putting a good edge on a blade is actually easy, and every woodsman should know the methods for both shop and field sharpening.

Never sharpen an axe or knife on an electric grindstone. No matter how careful you are in dipping it in water, you run the risk of burning the blade and taking the temper out of the metal. However, if you can find one of the old-fashioned foot- or hand-cranked "grindstones" that used to decorate Grandad's backyard, hang onto it. They make the best sharpening tool there is for almost any cutting edge from an axe to a pocketknife.

Sharpening axes. The first step in sharpening an axe is to file it. This should be done to a factory edge as well as the dulled edge of an old well-used axe. Place the axe head in a vise, or if you're in camp, extend the edge of the blade over the end of a stump or log. Use a good, medium-cut 8- or 10-inch file and, holding it flat, stroke from the eye out to the cutting edge. File only on the going away stroke, and keep turning the blade to file both edges evenly. The main thing is to produce a round edge, not a "wedge"-shaped edge. A wedge-shaped edge will have a tendency to do just that, wedge tight on a good hard swing, whereas a rounded shoulder will throw the chips outward away from the blade. To provide support, keep the cutting edge convex-shaped. An axe should never be "thinned" any more than when it comes from the factory, or the edge will break and chip easily. If you're reshaping or re-filing an old or badly abused axe head, start 2 or 3 inches back from the cutting edge and file up to the edge, cutting the old edge back to create a new one. File the axe in a fan shape, leaving a bit more metal at the corners for reinforcement.

Never sharpen an axe or knife blade on an electric grindstone; always file it. Even a new factory edge needs filing for a really sharp edge.

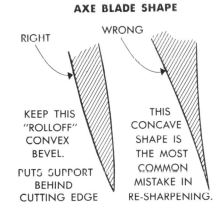

AXE BLADE SHAPE

RIGHT

WRONG

KEEP THIS "ROLLOFF" CONVEX BEVEL.

PUTS SUPPORT BEHIND CUTTING EDGE

THIS CONCAVE SHAPE IS THE MOST COMMON MISTAKE IN RE-SHARPENING.

When sharpening a double-bitted blade, many woodsmen like to file the two edges differently for a more versatile tool. One side is filed with an extremely rounded and shouldered edge and is used for splitting logs, hacking up large animal carcasses, and in general cutting where the blade is likely to come in contact with the ground, such as when cutting roots, etc. The opposite edge is sharpened at a more acute angle, honed razor sharp and can be used for anything from shaving

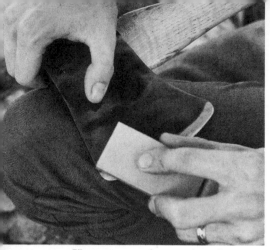

Hone an axe by moving the stone in a circular motion across the face of the blade, maintaining correct sharpening angle.

Light oil or a good rustproofing compound should occasionally be rubbed onto the head using fine steel wool.

to felling a huge tree. A good trick is to paint the blunt edge for easy recognition.

Once you have the blade shaped correctly and filed sharp, you should be able to sight down the edge and not see any bright or white spots. These indicate dull or nonsharpened areas. File them out. You will see a fine "burred" or wire edge which will require honing to remove. Using a fine, round emery stone, hone the axe blade razor sharp, moving the stone in a circular motion across the face of the blade. Other than sharpening, the blade needs little or no maintenance; a bit of light machine oil or rust preventive rubbed in with fine steel wool now and then will keep it free of rust.

Caring for the axe handle. The only other part of the axe requiring maintenance is the handle. It is held firmly in the head by wedges driven in the eye. The wedges may be seasoned hardwood or metal with wood-gripping edges. In any case, either are easy to replace. The woodsman can cut and replace wooden wedges while in camp. If a handle breaks and the end of the handle is pretty well wedged in the eye, cut off the handle up close to the underside of the head and drive out the remaining handle in pieces. Cut a new wedge of hardwood, tap the new handle in place and drive the new wedges home. A bit of the new handle and the wedge will protrude from the eye and should be cut off and the eye sanded smooth. Soaking the axe head in water will help tighten a loose handle, as the

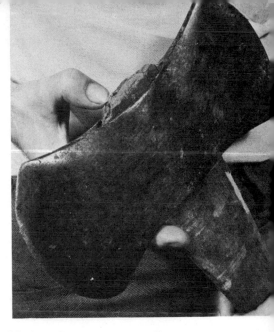

A badly abused, but correctable axe. Nails have even been driven in as wedges; head is still loose.

water swells the wood cells, but this is only a temporary fix-up until you get out of the bush and can get a new handle properly fitted in place.

Most manufacturers are now coating their axe and hatchet heads with a coating of plastic paint. This is great in several ways; it makes the axe easier to spot in brush or heavy under-cover, therefore less dangerous. It also enables you to spot a loosening handle immediately, because the paint will crack in the eye if the wood and metal gives in any way.

The handle should occasionally be sanded with fine sand-paper, especially if it becomes dampened and rough. Do not use steel wool, as you run the chance of leaving tiny fibers of steel which will cause rust spots in the handle and become embedded in your hands. Using a soft cloth, work linseed oil into the handle as a finish. Never use varnish or paint; you'll end up with a handful of blisters. A trick some woodsmen use is to bore a hole in the end of the axe, stuff it with cotton, pour in linseed oil, and carefully fit a wooden plug back in the hole. Never tape up a broken or splintered axe handle; replace it.

Many hatchets and single-bit axes come with a beautifully shaped fawn foot. Cut the tip of it off. In a pinch you can tighten a loose axe head by pounding on the foot with a ham-mer, or even a rock, and a sharp-pointed foot will merely break off, leaving you with a splintered handle. In zero or subzero weather, always warm an axe before starting to cut

FIXING AN AXE

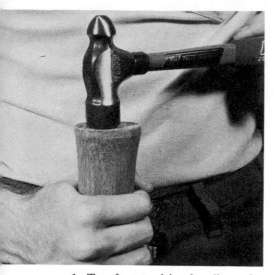

1. Tap foot to drive handle as far into head as possible.

2. Cut new hardwood wedges and drive in place.

4. The handle should occasionally be sanded with fine sandpaper.

3. Some of the wedge and handle will protrude from the eye of the head; cut it off with a coping saw.

6. Cutting the tip off of the fawn foot gives you a flat foot for easy tightening of the head, even using rocks available around campsite.

5. Rub linseed oil into the sanded handle with a soft cloth.

with it. Cold makes metal brittle, and the blade can snap unless warmed. After you start cutting, friction will keep the
blade warm enough. The best maintenance for an axe or
hatchet is the manner you use it, and every woodsman should
know the basics of good axemanship.

KNIVES

If I'm traveling extremely light or trail hunting, I don't carry
an axe or hatchet. I have a hunting knife made out of an
industrial file. The blade was purposely left thick and heavy
and sharpened with a wide angle so it can be used for chopping light brush or dead limbs for overnight camps. The un-
usually high carbon steel of the file makes a knife with an
exceptionally hard blade. It's the devil to sharpen, but will
keep an edge forever. It weighs only ounces as opposed to
my trail hatchet which weighs over a pound. I also carry an
old fashioned "Barlow" folding pocketknife that I keep sharp
enough to shave with, and that combination enables me to
handle almost any situation.

Many hunting and belt knives are designed for general purpose and are not even any good for that. You can't have a
perfect skinning, whittling knife, dagger and machete all rolled
into one. One of the biggest mistakes in buying a hunting
knife is buying a stainless steel blade. You can't sharpen it.

Three types of knife handles.

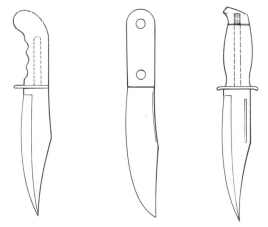

For trail hunting or other light-duty work, a heavy-bladed belt knife and an extra sharp pocketknife are an ideal combination.

There is absolutely no way you can hone an edge on it, the soft nickle in the steel will merely turn with the hone, giving you a rounded or burred edge. You can tell a good steel knife because it will darken with age, making it "blue" and practically rustproof. My handle preference runs to a wooden handle made of one of the heavy-oiled woods such as amaranth, teak or rosewood. These handles last longer than plastic, stag or leather, and when checkered with a coarse checkering pattern, really give you something to hold on to. The checkering should be no finer than 18 lines to the inch or it becomes mere deco-

A course-checkered wooden handle is one of the easiest to grip, and if made out of one of the heavy, oily woods is extremely long-lasting.

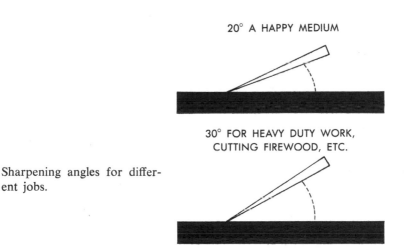

10° FOR LIGHT CUTTING
SUCH AS FISH FILLETING

20° A HAPPY MEDIUM

30° FOR HEAVY DUTY WORK,
CUTTING FIREWOOD, ETC.

Sharpening angles for different jobs.

ration and useless when the going gets rough. Once again the blade should not be filed concave (hollow ground), but with a rounded shoulder shape for support. However, the amount of sharpening angle depends on the type of knife. For a heavy-duty knife used more for chopping than slicing (such as the one I carry), an angle of 30 degrees is usually the best. A slicing knife, especially a fish-filleting or skinning and boning knife should have an angle of no more than 10 degrees. A general purpose knife can have an angle of 20 degrees.

Honing knife blades. To many people, getting a good edge on a knife is a mystery that went out with Daniel Boone. I've sat on my uncle's backdoor step and watched him hone his belt knife until he could take a hair and shave pieces from it. All it took was patience, time and several good stories. The problem today is that most of us just don't take the time to get

An excellent tool for restoring keenness to a blade is a good steel. Size shown is small and easy to carry on trail.

a good edge on a blade. An extremely battered knife will require a bit of filing to even up the blade and remove the nicks and dents. But for restoring keenness to a sharp blade, use only a hone or steel. A steel such as used by professional butchers and by farm wives for keeping butcher knives sharp is one of the handiest sharpening tools, and is now available in a small packable size. They just can't be beat for keeping knives sharp on the trail.

To hone an edge on any blade, oil the stone or lubricate it with spittle. Oil is the best and a stone oiled before you leave on a trip will keep fairly well. To maintain the proper honing angle for the type of blade you're honing, draw the blade edge first while sliding it across the stone. Or you can move the blade in tight circles, drawing it to you at the same time. Re-

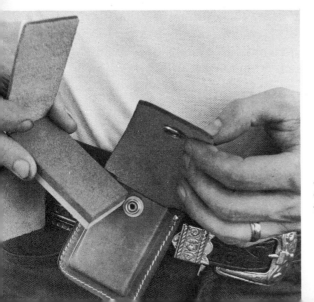

A small hone in a leather belt-case is also useful for keeping tools sharp in camp.

Leather handle on this small hone makes it ideal for sharpening small knives.

peat several times, counting your strokes, then turn the blade over and hone the other side with an equal number of strokes. The amount of pressure you apply is important. Start with a moderate to heavy pressure and finish with light strokes. If the blade is really dull, use the coarse side of the stone to develop a good angle on the edge before going to the fine grit. If the blade has only lost its keenness, it can be restored by using the fine side.

The main ingredient in a sharp blade is patience. Properly sharpening a knife takes a lot of time. Wipe the stone clean after each use. If it becomes filled with grit, clean it with lacquer thinner and a brush, then re-oil. Coarse filing or coarse honing will leave a burred or "white" edge along the blade when you sight along it into the light. Whet the blade until

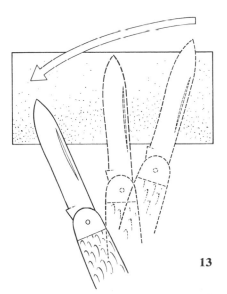

Proper honing stroke for small knife.

13

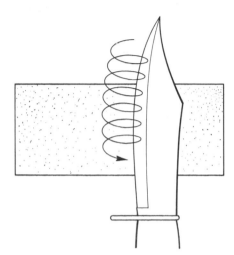

Proper honing stroke for large knife.

you remove all of this white area. Don't test the keen blade with your thumb as you have seen many drugstore whittlers do. Your finger probably won't be as calloused, and if you've properly honed the blade, you'll get a nasty cut. Instead, gently pull the blade across the back of your fingernail. If the blade pulls smoothly and slices a bit of nail easily, it's sharp. Another test: hold a piece of writing paper in one hand and slice the paper with the blade.

A truly keen blade will require stropping on a leather strop. The handiest strop a woodsman has is the inside of his leather hunting belt. Remove, stand on one end, hold the other and stroke the knife against the strop, this time pulling away from the blade edge. A strop for your shop can be made by gluing an unfinished piece of leather to a small board. For an ex-

Test a honed blade by dragging it across your fingernail, not your thumb.

A truly sharp blade requires stropping; one of the best strops an outdoorsman has is his leather hunting belt.

tremely sharp edge use the strop with jewelers' rouge. Drill a hole in the end of the board and hang it over your workbench. This will enable you to quickly strop your chisels as well as knife blades.

Replacing knife handles.   Knife handles are usually put on in one of three ways. One-piece handles of wood, bone, etc., are glued in place with epoxy. The blade tang is fitted up in a hole bored in the handle. Stag, leather rings, or plastic handles with a metal end cap usually are held in place by the metal cap being threaded onto the tang of the knife blade. A full blade knife has the blade extending completely through the handle and rivets holding the two-piece handles on. Brass rivets for these handles are available from mail-order houses and are easily punched out and reset for replacing broken handle halves. To replace a handle on a threaded-cap knife, place the knife (handle section) in a strong vise, one that is well padded with cloth or felt, and using a pair of water pump pliers (padded), turn the brass cap off the tang. Remove the cracked handle and replace. Once again this is usually a matter of drilling a hole for the tang to slip in, fitting the new handle in place and turning on the end piece.

SAWS

Although the camper or outdoorsman can get by with an axe, hatchet or even a heavy knife, a good camp saw is worth its weight in gold and will cut the time and effort required in gathering wood almost in half. A camp saw doesn't require as much skill to operate as an axe and isn't half as dangerous.

There are principally three kinds of camping saws. One is the bow saw, usually made of aluminum or steel tubing in a bow or modified V shape with the blade held in notches in the end. This is probably the most useful type of saw and the most popular. However, it is a bit heavier than other types and somewhat bulky. If you wish, you can simply remove the blade and pack it on your backpack. When you reach camp, you can easily make your own bow saw using just the blade, a bit of twine, rawhide, or wire and some saplings. The second type of saw is a folding saw that allows the "blade" to fold up into the handle like a giant jackknife. This is the easiest to carry, but not as good for cutting large-diameter logs. The third saw is really nothing but an unusual blade; it's like a piece of wire with finger loops on the ends. You can make a bow saw from it in the woods, or simply place your fingers in the loops and use it in that fashion. It requires no maintenance; you simply dispose of it when it becomes dull.

For light weight, blade from a bow saw can be removed and backpacked. Make a bow saw in camp from the blade, saplings and a piece of twine.

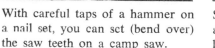

| With careful taps of a hammer on a nail set, you can set (bend over) the saw teeth on a camp saw. | Sharpening a camp saw is merely a matter of refiling the teeth, following their existing angles. |

A saw cuts because of two things: set of the teeth and sharpness of the teeth. In the usual crosscut saw blade found on camp saws, the teeth are set with each alternate tooth bent just a bit in the opposite direction so that when the cut is made in the wood the saw kerf is wider than the thickness of the saw blade, thus keeping the blade from being pinched and caught. The set in camp saws is usually quite a bit more pronounced than in shop blades because of their use on green and wet wood. As a rule, camp saws will not require a lot of resharpening work, merely filing the teeth with a fine triangle file to the existing angle, keeping all teeth the same angle and height. However, you may need to set the teeth a bit if the saw has been used on some hardwoods. You can do this with a hand-setting tool sold at most hardware stores, or if you're careful this can be done with a small ball peen hammer and nail set over the corner of a rounded anvil. The hardest thing on a saw blade is pinching it when sawing, and this can usually be prevented by preplanning of how the wood will fall, etc., also, you can use your axe blade as a wedge when sawing if you need to. Rust makes a saw blade drag, so keep the blade lightly oiled with light machine oil again applying with fine steel wool and wiping the surplus off with a soft cloth.

17

2 Canvas, Leather and Rubber

With the average sportsman, probably the most used and abused items are those made of canvas, leather or rubber. A pair of boots lasts until they wear out, maybe occasionally getting a new pair of laces or a coat of polish. If they're rubber, they probably last until the first hole, then are dumped. As for the fabric items—tents, sleeping bags, etc.—unless your wife is your hunting and camping partner, they really suffer. However, these items are actually the easiest to care for and, with today's modern materials, require the least amount of care or preventive maintenance of almost any equipment.

TENTS

Pitch your tent according to your manufacturer's instructions, not too tightly, not too loosely, just enough to remove wrinkles. Set too loosely, it will not shed water, but will hold "pools" which can eventually weaken the waterproofing or suddenly come sloshing down on you if you happen to brush against the tent just right. Pitching a tent too tightly stretches the seams, loosening the waterproofing there, and causes strain on the fabric and seam stitching. Always keep the tent in a protective bag or cover when not in use.

Storing tents. The hardest thing on any tent, from a heavy-duty car-camping tent to the lightweight nylon backpacker, is storing it while damp or wet. Mildew will invariably form on a tent stored damp or in a damp place, causing the material to rot and shorten the life of the tent. A mildewed item should be left to dry out in the hot sun, which kills the organisms. However, you will have unsightly black and gray splotches left after the organisms are dead. These can be removed by scrubbing with a mild solution of household disinfectant and water or bleach and water. The material is then hosed off to remove the bleach and stop the action.

Always dry your tent thoroughly before storing and keep it stored in a warm, dry, rodent-free area. If you must break camp while the tent is still wet, reset it when you get home and give it a chance to dry thoroughly. Don't pack wooden tent poles or stakes in the tent, as the wood has a tendency to hold moisture. Tie the wooden poles to the outside.

Cleaning tents.   Another essential maintenance with tents is to periodically clean them while camping. It doesn't take long to discover that although the sewn-in floor of most of today's modern tents has been the influencing factor in introducing the family to camping, the floors are a real dirt-catching nuisance. A toy broom can be kept with the tent if you're car camping, and the floor swept at campsite to remove the leaves, dirt and debris. If this debris is not removed, sooner or later it gets stuck to the inside of the tent roof, only to drop off in your face during a windstorm. An old throw rug positioned at the entrance to the tent will help preserve that portion of the floor and also cut down on the dirt. Brush off any bits of leaves or dirt from the bottom of the floor before folding the tent, as they will only stick to other portions of the tent as you fold it inward. Most experienced campers use a plastic tarp as a

At end of season, tent should be set up at home and given thorough cleaning, dirt and mud brushed off and dried mud hosed off.

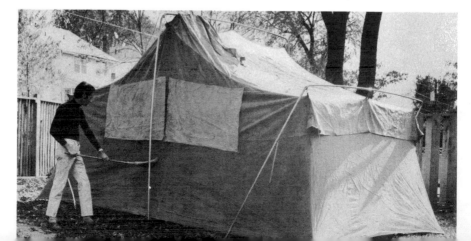

ground cloth before pitching their tent. This not only keeps the tent floor cleaner but gives it extra protection from rocks and small sticks that are likely to poke holes through the floor.

You should try to pitch the tent where there are no rocks or other sharp objects to puncture the floor, but this may not always be possible, especially if you have to pitch a tent at night by the headlights of a car. In any case, a few small pieces of "contact" paper available at the local dimestore will temporarily repair a small puncture hole in the rubberized flooring material. A better material, but one that doesn't look quite so good, is snips of black-plastic electrician's tape. This is one of the handiest things any camper can have in his repair kit. In a pinch it will temporarily "patch" almost anything. A more permanent patch for a tent floor is to use an iron-on pants patch or a piece of lightweight canvas, and cement it in place with either a canvas cement or, even better, an electric glue gun. The glue used in the glue guns is pliable and waterproof, and the heat needed to melt the glue gives a good bond with the flooring material.

Another cause of tent-floor damage is folding-cot legs. Although they are usually well-rounded on the ends, the leg ends are quite small in relation to the weight they distribute on the tent floor. The amount of pressure exerted on the cots can cause them to sink, especially if the ground beneath the tent is somewhat soft. A simple solution is to use a double layer of heavy corrugated cardboard beneath each cot leg (about 3 to 4 inches square).

Inside tent roof should be vacuumed to remove dirt.

Waterproofing tents.   Most modern tents are made of a good waterproofed material, and with normal use will not need an overall waterproofing for several years. Older materials may occasionally need to be rewaterproofed, and portions of new tents may require a "patch" job. Also, some waterproofing chemicals lose their effectiveness because of a chemical change brought on by mildew or mold action.

Waterproofing may be done in several ways, and using several different solutions. Spot waterproofing on seams can be done while in camp by simply rubbing beeswax to the underside of the leaking area until it starts to show light gray on the opposite side of the material. Or you may wish to use one of the new spray silicone water-repellent products. These new products are great for protecting both leather and canvas materials. The silicones penetrate the fibers without affecting porosity. The canvas and leather can "breath," yet keep moisture off. One application usually provides enough water protection for the season. For larger areas, or perhaps to do an entire tent, you'll want to use one of the more economical products.

There are bulk do-it-yourself waterproofing solutions available from almost any sporting goods store, department store or mail order house. These are merely painted on the pitched tent. In all cases, the tent should be completely dry, and the solution is applied wet enough to thoroughly saturate the material. Although there are many home recipes for tent waterproofing, most of them don't have the combined mildew-resistant, waterproofing action of the commercial solutions and are generally a waste of time. Also, many "home-brew" solutions are quite flammable when applied to a fabric.

Remember, your tent will repel water just as long as you don't touch the canvas from the inside during a rainstorm. If you do, the tent will start to leak exactly at the point touched, even if it is thoroughly waterproofed. The only solution is to move everything away from the drop and wait until the tent dries out.

Tears and small holes in tent flooring can easily be patched with snips of black plastic electrician's tape.

Lightweight nylon backpack tents may occasionally need to be waterproofed around the seams, especially at the stake cords and corners.

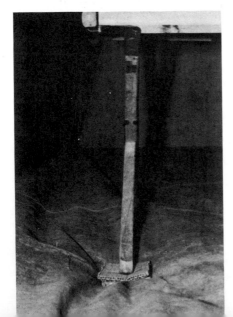

In camp, cot legs should rest on doubled layer of heavy corrugated cardboard.

 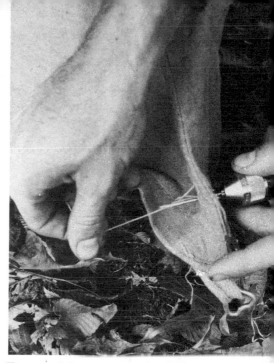

Small areas of tents can be water-proofed with silicone spray solutions. Entire tent should be water-proofed with more economical "brush-on" solutions.

Tears and loose seams should be patched as quickly as they're spotted with upholstery needles and heavy waxed thread, or by using an automatic awl.

Repairing tents. Tent tears and loose seams can easily be resewn with an upholstery needle and heavy waxed thread, or you can use one of the automatic stitching awls, as shown. They're great for sewing up anything from tents to boots. Repaired seams and tears should be waterproofed with a spray silicone waterproofing or by rubbing them with beeswax. Beeswax rubbed on the tent zipper will make it work better, especially in cold weather. However, a light spray with a silicone gun lubricant is best and will last longer.

One thing that is a must is to replace grommets as soon as they tear out. This is done with a grommet set that includes an anvil, punch and grommets of various sizes. The tenting material is positioned on a wooden block, the metal punch rapped to make the hole and the grommet bottom placed on the anvil through the hole in the material. The top portion of the grommet is placed over the bottom portion and the setting tool placed over the entire works and rapped sharply with a hammer.

23

HOW TO USE AN AUTOMATIC AWL

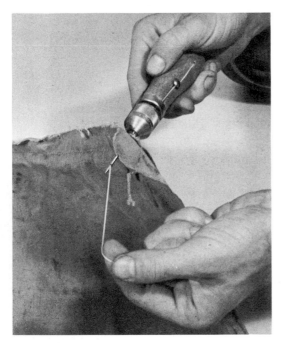

1. Pull out enough thread from inside the handle and through the needle to do the job. Then push needle through material and pull thread through entirely.

2. Pull needle back through, holding onto the thread. Then move about ¼ inch and push needle through again. Pull needle back slightly to start a loop and thread long thread through the needle.

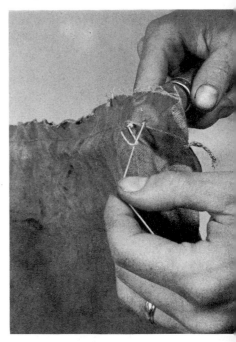

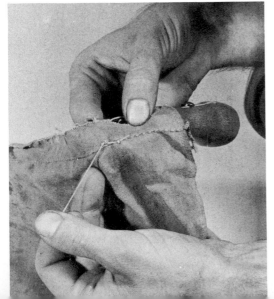

3. Pull the needle back through, holding onto the long thread, and you've made a loop stitch. Continue in this fashion until the area is re-stitched or patched.

Nylon tents. Very little care is needed for nylon tents. Once again the single most important thing is to let them dry out after use. Although nylon will not deteriorate with mildew, it will take on an odor. Nylon tents should be kept away from any intense heat or fire, and also strong cleaning solutions.

There is no need to clean the aluminum tent poles, as the dark gray is actually a layer of oxidation. When you clean it off, a new one will quickly form.

Resewn areas should be waterproofed with beeswax or spray waterproofing.

You can keep zippers in good working order by rubbing with beeswax or paraffin.

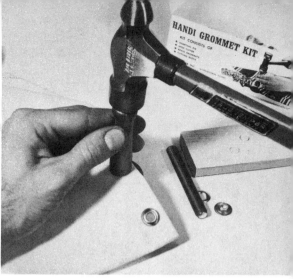

A grommet-setting kit enables you to quickly and easily replace grommets.

LEATHER BOOTS

As any "bird" hunter or backpacker knows, the shape of your boots in the morning will determine your shape in the afternoon. Leather boots require periodic care. They should be cleaned thoroughly and a good coat of waterproofing solution applied at least twice each season, preferably just before the season starts and once about halfway through. To clean boots of dried mud, use a dull putty knife or knife blade to gently scrape off any large chunks of mud and dirt, being extra careful not to gouge or "rough-up" the leather surface. Using a good grade of saddle soap and a soft bristle brush, thoroughly clean the boots. An old toothbrush can be used to work the lather down into the cracks and crevices. Make sure all dirt and mud is worked out. It may take several "latherings" to get the boots clean, particularly if they've been neglected for a couple of seasons. After the boots have dried somewhat, make up a lather of soft soap and neat's-foot oil, and work this mixture into the leather with your fingertips. Leave the boots in a warm spot overnight.

A bit of preventive medicine will help prolong the life of your leather boots. Be careful around salt spray, wiping it off at the end of the day and applying a coat of neat's-foot oil if the spray is excessive. If the spray is left on, it causes discolored spots and stiffens the leather. Many "dress" shoes have been ruined by the salt put on sidewalks in the wintertime to aid in walking on the ice.

Waterproofing leather boots. Most new leather boots today are waterproofed with a silicone solution at the factory.

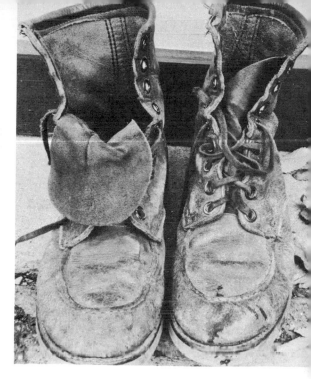

Typical pair of rundown but salvagable hunting boots. Lacing is broken and missing, leather has lost its waterproofing action, and some of the seams have come unsewn.

This does not make the boots completely waterproof but acts as a water repellent. Leather boots that are submerged in wet snow all day will eventually soak up moisture. This is to your advantage. The leather in a good pair of boots "breathes," allowing perspiration from your foot to escape, and your feet stay cooler in summer and warmer in winter. This is especially true if you wear a couple of pairs of wool socks with them.

Factory waterproofing will wear out in time and a new coat of waterproofing applied just before the season and during, as needed, will greatly help in keeping your feet drier in extremely wet walking conditions. In most cases, the waterproofing solution is a silicone-in-grease product and is applied heavily with the tips of your fingers, and not rubbed in. However, you must work it down into all seams and cracks. The boots are then placed in a warm spot such as a heat register or in front of a fireplace overnight. The heat causes the leather to soften and enables the waterproofing solution to "work" into the pores. It is also a good idea to apply a liberal coat of waterproofing to new boots. If you're renewing the leather tops of "pacs" or the New England type of hunting boot with leather tops and rubber bottoms, be sure that any leather conditioner or waterproofing solution you use is not harmful to rubber.

HOW TO REJUVENATE OLD BOOTS

1. Thoroughly clean the boots with mild soap, water, and soft brush.

2. Two or three coats of saddle soap and water is then used to further clean and soften the leather.

3. Apply a layer of Neatsfoot Oil and soft soap and work into the leather with the fingertips.

4. Waterproofing solution should be applied to old or new boots at the beginning of the season. It is put on heavy, not rubbed in.

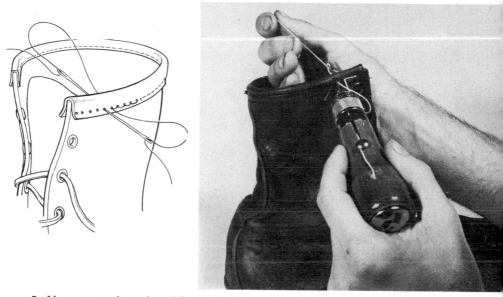

5. Use automatic awl and loop stitching to repair loose seams, or two needles as shown in drawing.

Drying leather boots.   Allow damp or wet leather boots to dry slowly, away from direct sources of heat such as near heat radiators or camp fires. If the boots are thoroughly wet and you need to wear them in the morning, hang them upside down a good distance from the fire. Although it has been suggested to stuff them with newspapers, this only impedes the air cir culation and slows drying. If boots are allowed to get too hot or dry too fast, the leather stiffens and the results are tiny cracks that shorten the life of the boots. When not in use, leather boots should be stored in a well-ventilated room at normal room temperature. If the storage area is too humid, such as in a basement or unventilated attic, mildew will form. This can be removed by setting the boots in the hot sun for an hour or two, then scrubbing with mild soap, again following with a leather dressing such as neat's-foot oil. Hunting boots generally have a bad name in the odor department. This can be remedied by sprinkling occasionally with powdered borax.

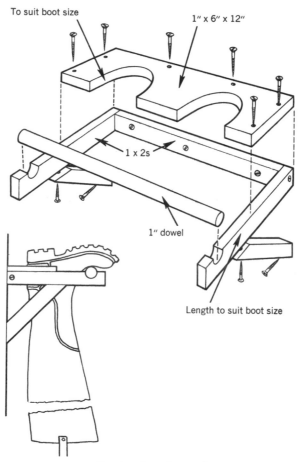

To suit boot size

1" x 6" x 12"

1 x 2s

1" dowel

Length to suit boot size

Boot and wader rack.

Repairing leather boots. Although resoling a hunting boot is beyond the average hunter's skills and ambitions, stitching loose seams is not. It requires only an awl, a couple of heavy needles and some waxed thread. You don't need to know a lot of "stitches." Just use the saddler's or harness stitch, as shown, using the two needles. Put the needles through the leather from opposite directions and tie off on one side. Or again, use one of the automatic awls and use the "loop" stitch, shown with the awl.

RUBBER BOOTS

There isn't much to repairing a pair of rubber hip or wader boots, but caring for them properly requires a bit of attention. They should be stored in a dry ventilated closet at room temperature and hung upside down by some sort of hanger as shown. Never leave them standing, folded, for very long, as this weakens the rubber at these points and continued use will cause it to deteriorate and separate. This is a particularly bad problem on chest wader boots where the heavy rubber material stops usually just above the knee. Rubber boots should not be stored in extreme temperatures; hot or cold hastens the rubber deterioration. Hanging rubber boots by their straps causes tension on the rubber by the weight of the heavy boot and again shortens the life of the boot. When the top holding straps wear out, they can be replaced with leather ones.

Repairing rubber boots.   Large rips or tears in rubber waders or boots are almost impossible to patch. However, pinholes and tiny snags are easily patched with an auto-tire patching kit. Some morning after putting out a decoy set you may crawl back into the blind only to find you have a tiny leak in one of your boots, and an extremely cold leg. Mark the boot with the hole and when you get back home hang it up outside and fill it full of water. In a few seconds you will notice a wet area seeping from the pinhole. Using a marking crayon, draw a circle completely around the hole, and large enough in diameter to stay out of your patch. Although most auto-tire patching kits come with a small metal tool for roughing up the rubber, do not use it on the boots. The rubber coating on the canvas is quite thin and you only make more pinholes. Instead, use a medium-grit sandpaper to roughen up the area around the pinhole. Spread rubber adhesive around the area and let it dry. Spread a couple of more coats, allowing each to dry. Select a patch, peel off the protective paper and press in place, burnishing it down with a pencil eraser or similar tool. Patches applied like this will stay on for several seasons. One of my hip boots has four patches that have been there through several duck seasons.

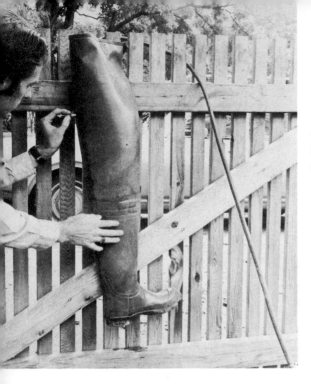

To find pinhole in rubber boots, hang up, fill with water and mark resulting leak.

Boots with an outside canvas surface such as many chest waders must be patched from the inside. This again can be a rubber patch, although the cement used must be a good canvas cement and the longest-lasting patch is actually one of rubberized canvas similar to the material in the boot. The main thing in patching this type of boot is to be sure and build up a good heavy coat of adhesive to make a smooth surface for the patch.

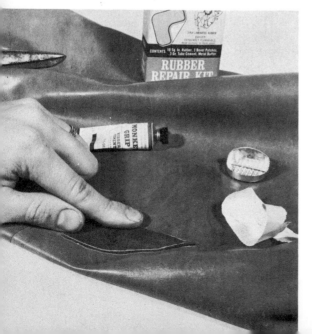

To patch rubber boots, use auto tire patching kit. Do not use metal roughing tool with kit. Instead use a piece of sandpaper to roughen area for applying adhesive.

SLEEPING BAGS

Much that applies to the care of tents also applies to sleeping bags. Above all, they should not be packed away damp or you'll have a mold problem. A good idea is to open them up completely and spread them out over a picnic table or clothesline for a couple of hours in the hot sun after each trip. This not only gives the material time to dry thoroughly, but also removes much of the odor that sleeping bags accumulate after a season. As for overall cleaning, read the label on your bag. Many synthetic fillings have to be dry-cleaned. Contrary to popular opinion, down-filled sleeping bags (down-filled garments too) do not have to be dry-cleaned. They can be washed in a home washing machine. Down is thoroughly washed four or five times by the processors before it is sold to the manufacturers. No additives are included and no cleaning fluids are used. The biggest problem in home washing is getting the down dry. This means five or six times more drying time in a spin dryer than anything you have ever dried before. The down will be matted and lumpy until completely dry. A warm temperature setting on the dryer will be the safest since excess heat may be injurious to both down and nylon. In the washing, you may have to hand scrub the dirtiest places around the hood zipper, etc.

Snags, tears or rips in sleeping bags should be repaired quickly, as they just keep tearing and pretty soon you have a real problem. In most cases, they can be resewn on a home sewing machine. If the down falls out, it may be stuffed back in place without any mess by using a vacuum cleaner backward, blowing the down into the channels. In case you lose the down or need a new supply, it is available through mail order in convenient "channel" pouches that enable you to "push" the down in place.

Zippers should be kept snag free and in good working order with an occasional light spray of silicone gun oil, or if you prefer, a light rubbing of paraffin.

MISCELLANEOUS

Leather belts, knife sheaths, bags and pouches can all be cleaned with the same techniques and materials as leather boots. Leather knife sheaths should also be thoroughly coated on the inside with a moisture-displacing spray such as a good gun oil. This does double duty of keeping the leather soft and the knife blade from rusting. Leather garments such as suede or buckskin hunting shirts and jackets require a few different techniques in care. They should be dry-cleaned at least once a year. For minor cleaning jobs, they can be cleaned with a damp sponge and a mild hand soap. Rub gently and dry the leather with a soft clean cloth. The leather can be dusted with baking powder to seal the pores, then wiped dry with a soft absorbent cloth. Many spots can be removed with an artist's gum eraser. Do not use saddle soap or shoe-cleaning preparations for garment leathers, as they tend to leave ring marks.

Duck or light canvas hunting clothing can be cleaned in the washer and dryer. However, "brush pants" with rubber knee pads will not come clean easily and shouldn't be washed in extremely hot water. Tears or rips in leather or canvas hunting clothes can be "patched" with iron-on patches applied to the underside of the material. Canvas hunting coats and hats can be waterproofed with spray-on waterproofing.

Many hunting shirts are wool and cannot be washed in hot water and automatic washing machines. They can be cleaned at home using cold water and wool-washing solutions or home-dry cleaning solutions. However, many of the new blends of fabric are hand washable. Check the label before cleaning.

Rubber air mattresses can be repaired with tire patching kits, or in some cases, with the patching kit that comes with the mattress. Rubberized canvas mattresses should be repaired with a canvas patch and canvas cement. The canvas patch should first be "waterproofed" by applying a coat of canvas cement to both sides and allowing it to dry thoroughly before adhering it to the mattress.

Canvas cots can also easily be patched with canvas patches and canvas cement.

Hats and hunting coats can be waterproofed with spray-on silicone and waterproofing solution.

Wool hunting shirts should be hand washed in cold water with wool-cleaning or dry-cleaning solution.

Canvas cots or rubberized-canvas air mattresses can be repaired with lightweight canvas patches and rubber canvas cement.

3 Camping Appliances

Yesterday's camping tools were sputtering and ornery; sometimes they worked and sometimes they didn't. Not today; with more and more people discovering the fun and excitement of living "outdoors," the list of camping tools has literally exploded. The new tools and outdoor "appliances" are extremely efficient, gaily colored and, best of all, dependable. A lot of research has gone into making this new equipment as trouble-free as possible. However, they still require a little care, as well as an occasional repair to keep them in their normal dependable and safe state. As a rule the repairs needed are so simple they can be done at campsite, and probably that's where 99 percent of them are done. On any camping trip, I carry a small tool and repair kit. It varies according to the type of camping. If I'm backpacking it may be nothing but a good pair of small side-cutter pliers, a small piece of copper wire, a few small nails, a roll of black plastic electricians' tape and a sharpening hone. If I'm boat or auto camping, I throw in a small socket set, a phillips and slot-head screwdriver, a spare lantern mantle, spare generator for lantern and stove, a lightweight hammer, and any spare parts such as outboard plugs.

LANTERNS

Usually the first outdoor appliance purchased by the camper is a lantern of some sort. It may be gas, propane, LP or even kerosene-fueled. In any case no matter what kind it is, it should be kept clean. Old, burned match heads should be kept out of the burner platform. The glass globe should occasionally be cleaned and the entire lantern kept clean of oil, dirt and spilled fuel. Always wipe your lantern after filling with fuel. This is not only a safe practice, but prevents dirt and grease buildup which may eventually cause operation problems.

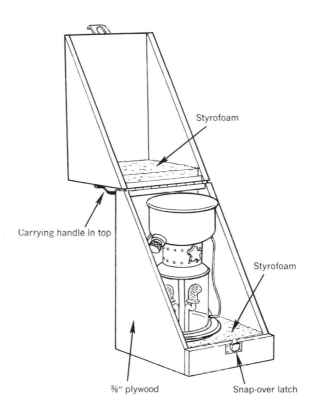

Styrofoam

Carrying handle in top

Styrofoam

⅜″ plywood

Snap-over latch

Case for transporting camp lantern.

Your lantern should be stored and transported in its shipping package, or in a box especially made for the purpose of carrying it. I like a lightweight wooden box for transporting and storing my lantern. Blocks of foam plastic in the top and bottom help keep the lantern in place and protect it from shocks. Never transport a lantern lying down, as you run the risk of breaking the mantle as well as spilling fuel and breaking the glass globe.

Always use the proper mantles for your lantern. It's a good idea to use the mantles called for in your owner's manual, or those sold by the same company that produced your lantern.

Many lantern users forget to turn the wire that cleans the generator tip. This wire should be turned as per your operator's instructions or it allows the tip of the generator to clog and makes the lantern hard to light.

These mantles have been tested and developed to produce the best results with their lanterns. Use the proper fuel. If your lantern is gas, use only clean, unleaded gasoline fuel or a good quality commercially packaged gas fuel.

Repairing lanterns. Normally a gas fueled lantern will give months, even years, of operation without so much as a few minor repairs. However, if it does start to give you trouble, there are several things to look for. If you have difficulty lighting the lantern, check the small wire handle that turns up and down. This cleans the carbon from the generator tip and many first-time users forget to turn it in the proper direction, and at the right time. The solution is to put in a new generator. If you can't keep pressure in a lantern or stove, check to make

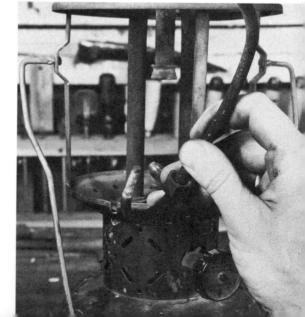

Occasionally you may need to replace a generator in a lantern. With the proper small wrenches it is an easy job.

Watch for cross-threading when turning gas bottles onto camping appliances. If you feel any resistance, stop and start again.

sure that the pump plunger turns down tight to seal off the pressure. If not, you may only have weak or stripped threads on the pump holder. If the leak does not seem to be in the area of the threaded holder, submerge the lower part of the unlit, cool lantern in a pan of water. If it has been pumped up and the pump is leaking, a small stream of bubbles will come from inside. In this case, take the lantern to your dealer for repair. If your lantern is properly pumped up, has plenty of fuel yet it burns with a weak yellow mantle, or with black spots on the mantle, check the air-supply screen in the tube above the mantle. Remove the mantle, brush the screen carefully with an old toothbrush and tie on a new mantle.

When the leather washer on a lantern or stove pump dries out it has to be oiled. A good indication of this is a pump that pumps "too easily." Use a light oil such as Neatsfoot oil or Sperm oil.

REPLACING A LANTERN WASHER

1. To replace a leather washer, turn the holding nut off using pliers and a small wrench; then remove the old washer to use as a pattern.

2. A good washer can be cut from the leather portion of an old shoe tongue. Use a sharp razor and cut it as accurately as possible.

3. Oil the leather washer and position it on the pump plunger. Fasten the holding nut back in place. If the leather is allowed to soak in oil for a few days, it will be a bit softer.

4. Place the new plunger in position and push it in. If you did your job correctly, it will be just a bit hard to push in, but within a short time, it will "shape" to fit the plunger tube walls and work easier.

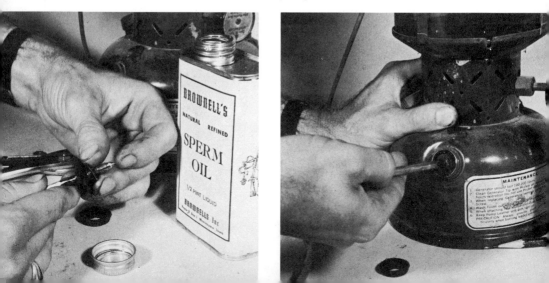

Storing lanterns.   If you are going to store the lantern for some time, fill the tank with clean, fresh fuel. Make sure the valve, filler cap and pump plunger are tightly shut. Place the lantern in a cool place. If the lantern is propane-fueled, remove the bottle and store it separately in a cool safe place. Although most manufacturers of propane-fueled appliances say to leave the propane tank in place until it is empty, I've found that unless you use the propane fuel manufactured by the same company that produced your unit, you may wind up with a poor fit and a leaky unit. Although the leak may not be enough to cause trouble at campsite, when storing or traveling in a closed car or station wagon with the stove or lantern buried under the gear in the back seat, it can be a bit irritating. On the other hand, never tighten gas containers onto stoves or lanterns with a wrench; turn to "hand-tight" only. If a bottle turns hard when you start it, stop and start again or you may ruin the threads by "cross threading" them.

Never use excessive force in tightening the valve, filler plug or pump plunger on a gas-fueled lantern. Tighten only to finger tight. Oil the pump leather at least twice each year. A few drops of motor oil or neat's-foot oil rubbed into the leather gasket is usually adequate. Frequently rotate the cleaning needle when the lantern is in use. This cleans the generator and keeps the gum and carbon deposits from forming on the generator tip opening.

Installing mantles.   Before you install new mantles brush the residue from the ends of the burner caps, using an old toothbrush or soft cloth. If the material isn't cleaned away from the mantle tube, it may fall down inside the new mantle when you tie it on. This debris not only won't burn, it may cause the mantle bottom to give way. For the brightest light, and for the most efficient burning, make sure the mantles are correctly installed. Place them in position and tie the drawstring securely around the mantle support, not the generator tube. Distribute the folds of the mantle evenly around the support and clip off the ends of the drawstring. Light the mantle and allow it to burn to a clean, white, ashy appearance. Always

HOW TO INSTALL
A NEW MANTLE

1. Before installing a new mantle, brush the dirt and debris from the air screen on the burner tube with an old toothbrush.

2. Position the new mantle in place and distribute the folds evenly around the mantle support. Do not fasten the mantle to the burner tube.

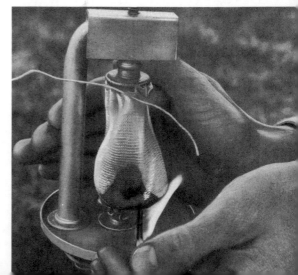

3. With the lantern in a protected area, light the bottom of the mantle and allow it to burn to a clean, white, ashy appearance. Replace the "globe" and mantle cap, and screw on the holding nut.

A gasoline-fueled stove can easily be converted to a bottled-gas unit with a conversion unit that installs easily in minutes.

do this in a quiet place, out of the wind, or you'll end up with a broken mantle and nothing but ashes blowing all over the place.

Always keep spare mantles on hand. Once you've made a trip and forgotten spare mantles, you probably won't forget them again. A package of spare mantles can be taped to the underside of most gasoline lanterns or kept with spare propane bottles. A good idea is to place mantles in strategic spots, such as in the automobile map compartment, or one in your fishing tacklebox, and don't forget to put one in your boat storage locker. Some outdoorsmen even like to lightly stitch one inside a hat or cap. Of course, they're left in their protective plastic bags.

CAMP STOVES

Use only clean, unleaded gasoline fuel, or a good grade of packaged fuel. Otherwise you may end up with a clogged generator orifice. Clean your stove after each use. Match heads or other foreign particles around the burner head will cause smoky tongues of yellow flame, an inefficient and wasteful use of fuel. Grease and dropped food particles should be cleaned away from the burners, and also out of the bottom of the stove. Aluminum foil positioned under the grill and around the burner will not only make cleanup a snap, but will reflect a great deal of heat to produce a hotter flame, quicker.

Dirt and grease are the villains with any camping stove. Grease eventually plugs the gas opening and stops the fuel from coming through. Keep the stove clean by wiping down after each trip with a damp rag.

Removing grease. Grease is the prime villain in keeping stoves in working order and particularly in the propane or LP fueled units. The tiny orifices quickly become clogged and stops the fuel flow to the burner. If this happens in the field, remove the tiny brass orifice by turning it out by hand, reverse it end for end and hold it tightly against the end of the tank valve. With a short burst of fuel from the bottle, "blow" the obstruction from the tiny port. Naturally, do this in an area where there is no flame. If this doesn't work, you'll probably have to soak the clogged orifice in a jar of lacquer thinner for a day or two, then carefully dry it off and again try to blow the obstruction from the port. Do not use a pin point or tiny wire to attempt to clean the opening. You'll only damage and further clog the tiny brass port. If you're unsuccessful in cleaning the orifice, order a replacement. In fact, it's not a bad idea to have one or two on hand.

When an orifice does become plugged, turn it out, hold it in place backwards, and give it a short burst of the gas. If this doesn't clear it, soak it in lacquer thinner for a couple of days, then try again.

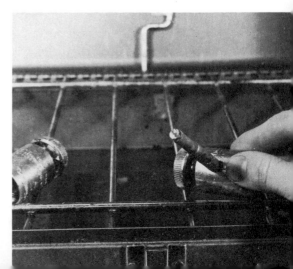

Miscellaneous maintenance.   Do not use force in tightening the valve or filler cap. The stove will burn several minutes after the master valve is closed.

If the stove is to be stored for some time, fill the tank with clean, fresh fuel. Make sure the valve, filler cap and pump plunger are tightly closed.

At least a couple of times a year remove the pump plunger and oil it with a couple of drops of clean motor oil or neat's-foot oil. If the plunger leather is badly deteriorated, replace it with a new one cut from the tongue of an old leather shoe. The new gasket should be softened with neat's-foot oil for a couple of days before installing on the plunger.

The stove should be kept in a protective case while transporting or storing. The shipping container in which the stove came makes one of the best carrying cases, so keep it, don't throw it away.

The job of the generator on a stove or lantern is to change the liquid fuel into a vapor. Eventually the generator tip may become so filled with carbon that no fuel can be forced through it. Always keep a spare generator on hand and change it if the carbon becomes too bad. A generator should last for at least 100 hours of operation, longer on new stoves.

You should also frequently check the gasket in the filler cap and replace it with a new one cut from sheet cork when needed. The tank should occasionally be cleaned by rinsing it with clean fuel and dumping the washing fuel out, then adding clean fuel for burning. If you have a gasoline stove, it can easily be converted to propane with a conversion kit that installs in less than a minute without the use of tools.

On camp stoves from which the fuel cylinder must be removed before collapsing the stove, be sure the valve on each cylinder is shut. If cylinder removal is not necessary, leave them in place until the gas supply is exhausted. However, you may discover that not all cylinders and stove valves will fit tightly. In this case, remove the bottle after using the stove, otherwise you'll end up with an empty bottle, or one leaking out into your car. As butane cartridges do not have shut-off valves, they must be left in place.

Most propane cylinders are equipped with a safety-relief valve. If exposure to extreme heat causes the container pressure to increase, the relief valve opens automatically, dissipating this pressure safely. Excess gas seeps through the valve as a liquid, then vaporizes immediately. When pressure is back to normal, the valve recloses. To prevent this gas leakage, spare propane cylinders should be stored in a cool place.

Catalytic heaters have been a blessing to all outdoorsmen who enjoy winter outdoors. Unlike camping lanterns and stoves, they should not be stored with fuel in them.

CATALYTIC HEATERS

Once again, use only the fuel specified by the manufacturer. Never use cleaning fuel to clean the head; this only contaminates it and can clog the head and prevent it from working.

The rule for storing a catalytic heater is the opposite from that for stoves and lanterns. It should never be stored for any length of time with the fuel in the fount. The heater should be stored in a wooden box or its shipping container, and kept upright at all times.

JUGS AND COOLERS

Jugs, coolers and "Thermos" bottles should be thoroughly washed after each use, rinsed inside and out and left to air out in sunlight for an hour or so after each cleaning. A bit of baking soda dropped in a damp bottle or jug will sweeten it and remove any left-over odors. The baking soda should be left in for about an hour, then rinsed out with clean water.

Be extremely careful of plastic coolers when dragging them on sand or gravel sandbars and beaches. If you store them on a concrete garage floor, make sure there are no sharp objects or stray rocks that can work through the fragile plastic.

Also be extremely careful when using an ice pick or hunting knife to break up chunks of ice inside the cooler. However, if you happen to slip and jab a hole in the side of the cooler, it can easily be patched. On older coolers, the inside metal liner can usually be patched with plastic aluminum or a tiny spot of solder. Make sure the area is clean and well smoothed with either fine steel wool or sandpaper before applying either. Small holes in the newer plastic-lined coolers are also easy to fix. Merely dab the hole with fingernail polish until you build up the hole and fill it in. Do not use household glues, as some adhesives will injuriously attack the plastic liner.

Coolers should occasionally be washed with a rag dampened with water and dipped in baking soda. Allow them to air dry between trips with the lid partially open.

An ice-pick hole can be repaired in plastic coolers using a bit of clear nail polish to build up the damage. In metal cooler liners, use plastic metal or a bit of solder.

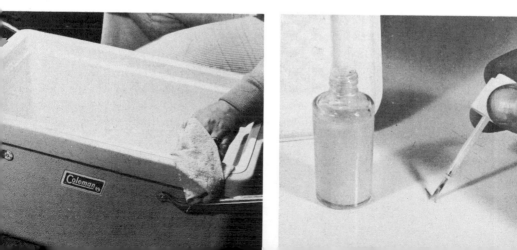

Cooler hinges should be lubricated with a light lubricant such as penetrating oil.

Talcum powder dusted on the rubber seal of a cooler edge will give it longer life, keep it from sticking in hot weather.

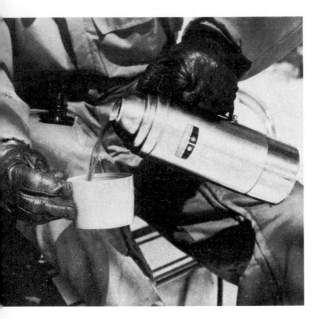

One of the easiest items to maintain is a stainless-steel Thermos. Between trips it should be left open to air out. Like a cooler, it can be freshened with baking soda.

Always allow the cooler to air out for some time after each trip with the lid open. This allows the interior to stay fresh and sweet-smelling, ready for the next trip.

Check hinges on ice chests and apply a few drops of oil on them. Also check the catch to make sure it holds the lid tightly in place. Cornstarch or talcum powder sprinkled lightly on the rubber gasket will help keep it from getting sticky.

COOKING UTENSILS

Camp cooking utensils should be washed right after using. A lazy man's way is to place a kettle of water on the fire as you take off the food to eat. Also pour a bit of water in the skillet and place it on the fire with just a drop of dish soap. By the time you've finished your meal, the water is hot, so you drop your plates and utensils in the hot water and they will come clean quickly and easily. If your water is hot enough, you won't even have to dry the dishes. Just place them on a table or cloth and allow them to dry from their own heat.

Modern-day technology is finding its way into the camper's cookbox with Teflon-coated cookwear. It's as easy to care for in the wilderness as in the home.

Aluminum utensils. The outsides of aluminum utensils such as coffee pots or nested cook sets quickly become covered with black soot. You can prevent this to some degree by covering the outsides with soap. You can easily clean this "cooked-on" covering by washing the pots in hot water to which dish soap and a bit of TSP (trisodium phosphate) have been added. This is pretty strong stuff, so use either rubber gloves or a plastic swab. Use scalding hot water to thoroughly rinse and clean the solution from the metal to stop the cleaning action. An even lazier method is to leave the black. Make cloth sacks to hold the cook kit, coffee pot, etc., and place them in these sacks for traveling. Wipe the excess black off with a paper towel or newspaper before putting them in the sacks. You can then scour the pots at home if you wish.

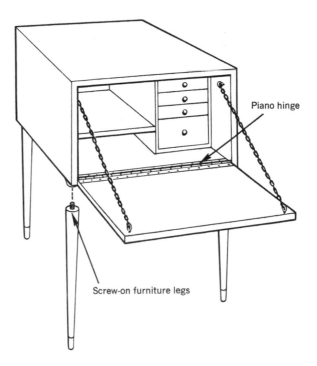

Piano hinge

Screw-on furniture legs

Camp cupboard for neat storage of food and cooking utensils. Build it to your own dimensions.

Discarded refrigerator grate makes a good campfire grill. Transport it in a canvas sack so it won't soil other gear.

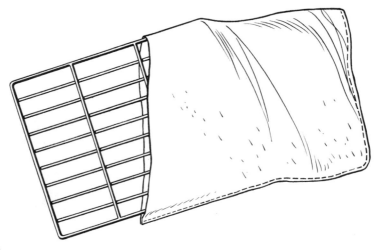

Dutch ovens and cast iron skillets.   These must be broken in and cared for in a somewhat special way. Old-timers use bacon fat and heat the new skillets smoking hot, then rub the chunk of fat around the skillet to break it in. A clean dry cloth is then used to swab the excess lard out. To clean a skillet, heat it smoking hot, and again a chunk of bacon fat and a clean cloth. This protects the metal from rusting and eventually pitting.

An old refrigerator grate makes an excellent "campfire" grill. Most camping spots have enough loose rocks lying around so that you can make a "circle," or just prop the corners up away from the firewood. The grill can also easily be cleaned of the grease and soot by scrubbing it with soap and TSP solution. However, this is done easier at home, and for transportation, the "dirty" grill can be put in a canvas sack especially made for keeping the grill from soiling other camping items. It should be noted that food should never be cooked directly on a refrigerator grill. If you like to grill steaks on your outings, save the grill from that old barbecue.

BACKPACKS, FRAMES AND BASKETS

Although aluminum backpacks can be cleaned and brightened with a mild solution of cleaner as used for the cooking utensils, your best bet is to leave the aluminum alone. It will only oxidize again, almost immediately after cleaning.

A frame that is bent can usually be straightened, if you work carefully. Be careful not to bend the frame too much in the opposite direction or you run the risk of snapping it off at the weakened bend area. A broken frame can be spliced with short pieces of do-it-yourself aluminum and a couple of "pop rivets." However, a broken frame is an unusual case.

Canvas and nylon pack sacks can easily be repaired with cloth-mending cement and patches of suitable material glued in place. Long rips may necessitate sewing the patch in place as well.

Pack baskets are usually made out of hickory splint and need to be occasionally revarnished to protect them from moisture.

Aluminum backpacking frame can be repaired by using a pop-rivet gun and a lightweight aluminum splice.

Use only an exterior varnish of a good grade. Split rims and cracked strips on pack baskets can be held together with a wrapping of soft copper wire. However, this is only a temporary job, and you'll need to replace the busted members when you get home.

Always check the pockets of your packs for crumbs before storing for material that might spoil or draw pests.

4 Fishing Tackle

No matter whether you pursue "hog" bass, lunker trout or slab-sided crappie, at the end of the fishing season, your equipment is usually in shambles. Lures are a tangled and rusty mess. Your rod has a loose guide or ferrule, and your tacklebox is a complete tangle of lures, snips of line, mud and scum, leftover candy wrappers, and watersoaked book matches. In fact, one of my worst habits is leaving my tacklebox spread open in the boat in front of me. This allows water dripped from lures, off battling fish or from light rain to get into the box and equipment, and induces general havoc by being a good place to "throw" trash and junk to keep it from blowing out of the boat. Unfortunately, I also throw the lure back in the box in my hurry to change to another lure and get back to fishing.

At end of heavy fishing season, tacklebox, lures, rods, and other equipment are in bad need of organizing and repair.

The best care you can give your equipment is to have a safe, easily reachable place to store each item whether it be rod, reel or lures. Unfortunately, there isn't a tacklebox made that's big enough to hold all the fisherman's equipment. If I had a steamer trunk fitted with casters and handles, it would be full of plugs and equipment. The only solution is organization. Then sometime you've got to stop and take stock of what you're missing and start fixing up repairable equipment.

LURES

The best place to start rebuilding the havoc is with your lures. Clean and repair them each season. Not only will you be able to spot and pick them up easier when cleaned and shiny, but they will have much of their same brightness and fish-attracting appeal as when new.

Spread some old "white" wrapping paper on a basement or garage floor and dump the entire tacklebox out. Don't use newspaper, as you may miss picking up a hook or two, which can be hazardous to pets or tires. Sort out your lures and tackle, organizing and putting hooks and sinkers, etc., in their plastic boxes, or in individual piles. Sort out and untangle the plugs and lures, placing those that need to be repaired in one pile, and those that need only to be cleaned in another.

Cleaning plugs and lures. Those that are mildly dirty can be cleaned with ordinary dish soap and a soft cloth. They should then be dipped in clean water and wiped dry. However, for extremely dirty plugs, or to remove water scum and give a better sheen to spinners and spoons, clean them with a good household silver polish. Use just a small portion of polish on a soft cloth, then dip plug or lure in water and buff with a clean soft cloth. If rubber skirts are soiled and dirty, replace with new ones. Feather or bucktail lures can be rejuvenated by holding momentarily in the steam from a teakettle, then re-shaping with fingertips. For a more thorough cleaning job, as well as to prevent pricked fingers, it's a good idea to remove hooks while cleaning.

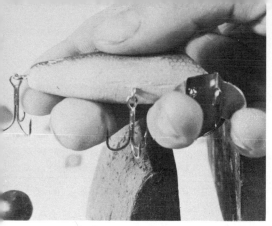

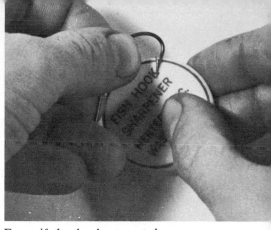

Easiest repair job on lures is simply to replace rusted and dull hooks with new needle-sharp ones.

Even if hooks have not become rusty, there's a good chance they're pretty dull, and can be the edge a big fish needs to win the battle. Sharpening takes but a few minutes with a tacklebox-size hook hone.

Dish soap and warm water will clean most of the dirt and scum off lures.

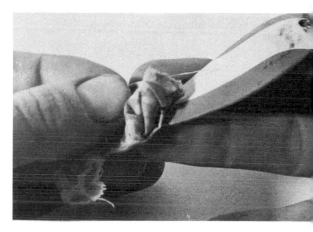

Chrome- and silver-plated spoons, as well as many other shiny lures, are best cleaned with a small portion of household silver polish.

Some plugs merely require slipping a new skirt onto tail.

Replacing hook.   This brings up the next step. Unless the hooks are sharp and rust-free, they should be replaced with new ones of the same size and shape. Replacing hooks is a comparatively easy task. On plastic and wood plugs, they are held in place by small "closed" screw-eyes threaded into the plug. You can purchase both the tiny (open) screw-eyes in most sporting goods stores and the hooks in the size and conformation needed for the lures. Turn the new screw-eye in the plug, place the hook in position and lightly squeeze the screw-eye closed with a pair of needle nose pliers. Turn the hook and eye a couple more turns to keep the eye from opening. New hardware can also be purchased for almost any type of lure from the gurgling, sideways working lip of a surface lure to the "shovel" of a deep runner. These are usually held in place by tiny screws furnished with the hardware.

Repainting plugs and lures.   If you have a favorite plug that has been chewed and mangled in battle, don't give it up. There is probably a good reason for its success. It has that "something special" action that attracts strikes and a new one of the same type may not work as well for you. If the plug has deep gouges, you can patch it with either wood putty or "epoxy" two-part glue. Carefully sand the patched portion down to the surrounding surface. Be extra careful to keep the "character" of the plug the same as before. Using fine sandpaper or steel wool, smooth the finish down to a soft sheen. Suspend the plug, by a screw-eye and paper clip, in a cardboard box, and spray it with several coats of a good "enamel." The base coat should be white on all multicolored lures. After the last coat, knock down the rough spots with extremely fine sandpaper. Depending on the type of plug, it should be painted in the pattern best suited to it.

If you intend to paint the plug in a scale finish, it should be undercoated in a rough pattern of different colors. For instance, on lures resembling bait fish, the top is usually painted green or black, sides a pale green, and front of the head or "mouth" a deep red. Feather the edges of the colors into each other. In most cases, the belly is left white. While this is drying, fasten a small piece of scale netting or, as it's called in fabric stores, "nylon netting" to a small wooden frame. Do not stretch the net too tightly, but apply it in a loose fashion. (when you place the lure against it for spraying, you will get a better contact all around.) Position the frame in some sort of holder or vise, press the side of the lure close up against the netting, hold it firmly in position and spray a light dusting coat of either silver or gold enamel. When this has dried, turn the lure around and spray the opposite side. The result is a professional-looking scale finish that you will be proud of. When you've used the net for quite a bit, the tiny holes become clogged and scales uneven. Throw the netting away and start with a new piece.

New eyes can be painted on a lure by dipping the end of a small dowel into enamel and pressing a tiny "dot" of paint in place. The size of the end of the dowel is shaped with a pencil sharpener. The eye looks most natural with a large dot of white; then when this is dry, apply a smaller dot of black in

For a complete rejuvenation of plugs, remove hooks, apply several coats of paint in pattern desired.

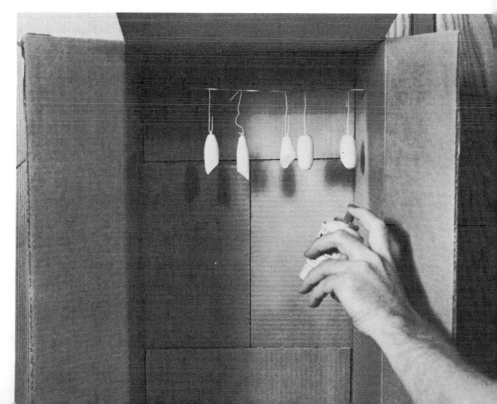

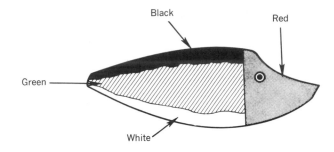

Black

Red

Green

White

A base coat of paint is applied, then various colors are sprayed on back, belly and sides as shown in drawing.

To produce a scale finish on a lure, staple a piece of netting to a small wooden frame. Hold the lure firmly against netting and spray with paint. Resulting scale finish is shown at right.

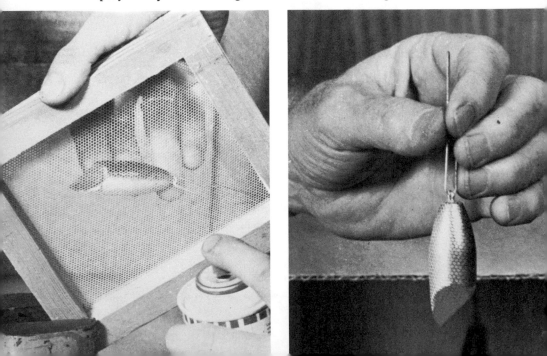

Eyes or "frog spots" can be applied with small dowels dipped in black and white paints.

Finished lures can be given added protection and waterproofed by dipping in clear Epoxy finish or a quality spar varnish.

Some plug designs do not require scale finishes. They look best when dipped in paint.

Refinished plugs with new hooks are a great saving.

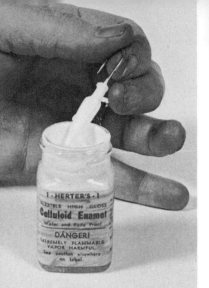

Jigs are easily repaired by dipping in paint, then tying on bucktail or marabou dressing.

Spinning-lure blades and lead bodies also can be repainted for a fresh, new look.

the center of the white one. "Dowel dots" also are an easy method of applying "frog" spots to surface lures. Use at least a couple of different sizes of dowel ends and vary the pattern with big and little spots. Place most of the larger dots on the top or upper portion of the lure.

60

With a wire-bending tool, you can repair and rethread damaged spinning lures.

Although most good spray enamels will withstand the water and abuse of fishing conditions, a good extra bit of protection is provided by dipping the plug or lure into a can of clear epoxy finish, or spar varnish. Hang it up to drain off, and wipe off any "blob" of finish that forms on the lower end as the finish dries. Some plugs, particularly those popular "red-and-white" plugs can be repainted by dipping a white-base-coated plug into a can of red enamel at a slight angle, then hanging it up to dry.

Lead-heads and jigs have a tendency to become chipped and worn with very much use. A simple remedy is to clip off the chewed and frayed feather or hair wrappings and dip the jig into enamel. When it is dry, tie on a new feather or hair wrapping. The same goes for spinner lures with lead or metal bodies. They become chipped and a fresh coat of paint can often make them look like new. However, if the metal shaft is bent or damaged, it should be replaced. This is an easy job if you have a wire-bending tool for working with fishing-lure wire. A new shaft is made, the parts threaded in place and an eye closed on the opposite end. A trailer hook sometimes covered with hair or feathers usually is attached with split rings.

Storing lures. Leave a compartment in the tacklebox for each lure, particularly if the lures are large or have a double set of treble hooks. This not only prevents damaged lures, but damaged tempers as well. A few years ago when plastic worms were introduced, they were, and in some parts of the country still are, the hottest fishing lure on the market. The "old worms" had one fault; they melted practically every plastic plug or the finish on every wooden plug they came in contact with. Today that is seldom the problem it used to be, but plastic worms are still the hardest-to-store item. They slip down into crevasses, pick up the least amount of dirt and oil, become entangled with treble hooks almost on contact, and then become useless themselves as fishing lures. Most fishermen today use the worms in a "slip-sinker" method rather than rigging them with hooks and harness as was the former method. For storing the rigged worms, the only solution is to snitch the kids' clear plastic pencil box. Unrigged worms—and if you bass fish very much you'll have quite a color assortment—can be stored in small plastic bags tied with wire ties. Place different colors in separate bags, along with an equal amount of egg sinkers, and you're ready for action. You can also place them in small baby food jars, and with the lid on they're safe and protected.

RODS

You've packed into some remote mountain lake and on about the third or fourth cast you snap the tip off your rod. "This rarely happens," you say. You bet it does—it happened to my wife last summer. She was lucky, there was a spare rod nearby. Although the rod she was using was several years old, it was a quality brand-name rod and it broke for no apparent reason. She didn't strike it against an object or have the tip under any leverage.

There are several precautions against this possibility. One, you can pack along an extra rod, but usually if the fishing is good, it's in a pretty remote area and any extra weight can be quite a burden, so you elect to leave it at home. Second, you can always carry a rod repair kit with you. One such kit, consisting of two short lengths of aluminum and some plastic tape, is available from the Gudebrod Company. This handy item won't leave your rod in ideal fishing action, but it will keep it fishable.

Replacing the tip. If just the top few inches of the tip break off, you can repair it with a pocket knife, a match and some ferrule cement. Using a match or pocket lighter, heat the tip and tip guide until you can work the tip guide loose. This may take a bit of time, but be patient. Some tips are not put on with ferrule cement, and won't react to the heat. In this

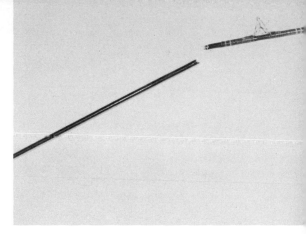

A broken rod tip can be bad news, especially if you've packed in to some remote fishing area.

case, break off the tip and dig out the fiberglass splinters with a sharp knife. If you have a fast-action tip, and it's broken off some distance down, the tip guide will not fit down over the broken rod end. The solution is to use your pocket knife to gently "flare" the end of the guide to fit the rod end. Square up the rod end and make sure everything fits. Warm up a bit of ferrule cement, place it on the rod tip and force the guide in place. Not the best-balanced or best-looking rod, but it will do in a pinch. If you bought your rod from a reputable dealer and it's a good brand name, you can usually get a replacement tip at a small cost. However, you may do as I once did and discover a "custom" rod by this accident. I now have a shortened spinning "boat" rod that is excellent for nighttime fishing. It's shortened length is great for working in close to shorelines, and it is an "ultra-stiff" spinning rod for horsing those lunker bass out from the log jams they seem to favor.

In a pinch, you can remove the tip guide and replace it on the shortened rod.

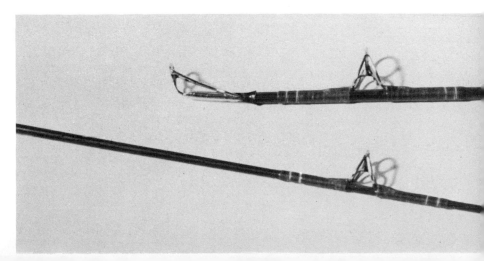

Replacing the grip.   With hard use, cork grips have a way of deteriorating in a few years on even the best of rods. However, they're easily replaced. With spinning rods, you will likely have the hardest job. The handles are glued on with a heat-working, waterproof glue and when they have become broken will have to be cut with a sharp knife and chisel. The rod blank will run the entire length of the handle and the exposed blank should be lightly sanded. To replace the handle with a "preshaped" spinning handle, you will have to remove any guides on that portion of the rod, as the handle usually has to slide down over the small end of the rod, and be slightly forced down on the tapered "butt" end. A thorough coating of waterproof glue is applied to the rod butt before applying the handle. Some fly rods and spinning rods have the handle held in place by a butt cap and can be removed from the butt end after first removing the cap. Most spin-casting and bait-casting rod cork handles are held in place by a metal butt cap "washer" and screw. Remove the screw and washer. Cut the damaged handle off and glue on a new preshaped cork handle or cork rings with waterproof glue, replace the washer, tighten the

Broken and deteriorating rod handles can be replaced with cork rings or a preshaped cork handle.

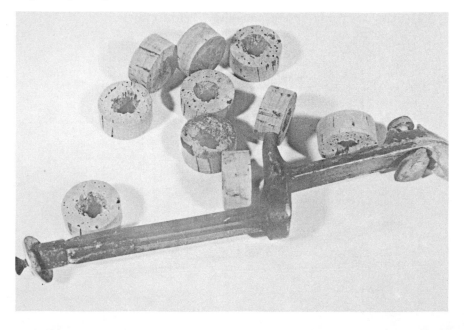

Handle is rasped, filed and sanded to the shape desired.

Rings are lathered with waterproof glue, threaded on rod and squeezed together by screw and rod cap. Rod should be left in warm place overnight.

Preshaped handles, with reel seats for spinning reels, are merely slipped on rod, glued in place.

rings in place with the screw and leave in a warm place overnight. If you used the rings, you will have to shape the handle as desired. Usually the cork ring holes will not exactly fit the handle, and will require boring out for a press fit. This is done with a variable-speed portable electric drill or hand drill and wood-boring bits. Soaking the cork rings in boiling water before boring them will keep them from splitting. If the butt tip is deteriorating and it has no cap, a crutch tip can be slipped over it.

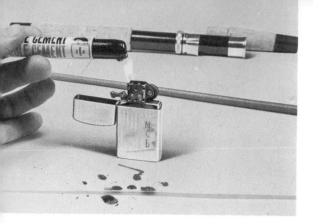

For repairing ferrules, ferrule cement is warmed with match or pocket lighter.

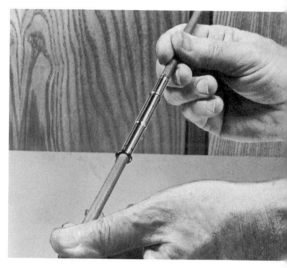

Drops of cement are placed on rod blanks and ferrules positioned together, pushed in place.

Replacing ferrules. If a ferrule comes loose, it can be replaced with ferrule cement. The cement is heated to "melt" it into drops which are quickly smeared on the rod blank. The rod blank then is quickly forced into the ferrule and held into position until the cement sets. Excess cement can be trimmed off with a sharp knife. Some ferrules are a bit smaller on the end next to the rod blank. On these you can wrap a winding identical to the guide windings, continuing it up onto the rod. This provides more strength for holding the ferrule in position.

If the ferrules on your rod fit too tightly, very lightly touch them with steel wool to remove any caked-on grease or dirt spots. Then apply a tiny bit of reel lube grease to make them work easier. To fit on a new tip, you may have to crease it a bit with a dull blade to get it to crimp down onto the tiny rod tip.

Replacing guides. While it looks quite complicated, winding on new guides is easy and a sure way of rejuvenating your favorite old wand. You can buy replacement guides in almost any size or quality, or you can merely rewind those from your old rod. Before putting on new guides, one step ensures they will fit your rod better and produce a tighter-fitting, better-looking winding. Gently mash their tips to fit down flat on the rod surface. If they're plated, be careful not to break off the plating.

A couple of economical, homemade tools will help a great deal in rewinding a rod. A wooden rack shaped like an upside-down foot stool, with notches in each end, will do nicely for supporting the rod while you turn on the windings. Another handy helpmate is a "bobbin" made of a twist of wire and a bolt and nut. Twist a loop in the middle of the wire, then bring it down on either side of a spool of winding thread. Form it around a bolt on either side of the spool and gently tighten a nut on the bolt until the bobbin will hang in mid air without unspooling the thread.

Tape one end of the guide in place and, starting on the guide, wind outward, covering the beginning end of the thread to secure it. You can wind on the thread in any pattern you choose; using variegated thread for a varying pattern, tying off

Rewinding and replacing new guides is easier with a rack to hold rod in position.

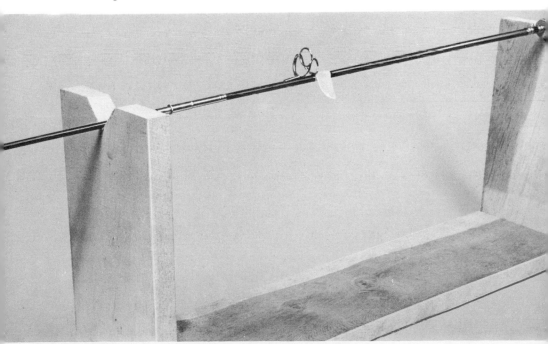

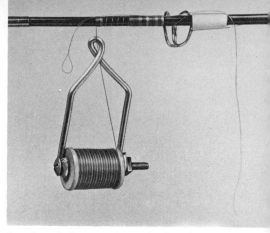

For the best appearance, guide ends should be lightly flattened so winding can cover guide ends easily.

Another helpmate for winding is homemade bobbin of wire and bolt.

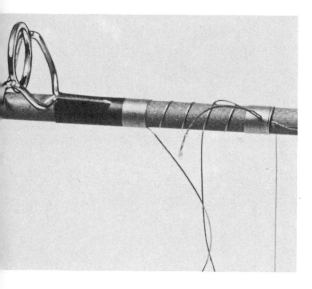

To tie off winding, a loop of fishing line is positioned along rod, winding continued over it. End of winding is placed through loop, loop pulled back under winding.

To preserve bright colors of winding threads, first cover with fixative or fingernail polish.

Last step in repairing rod is to apply several coats of rod varnish. Allow each coat to dry thoroughly before applying next.

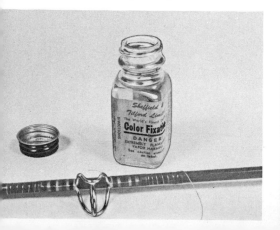

and starting different colors in different patterns, or even winding in silver thread for emphasis. No matter what pattern you choose, make sure you repeat it in the opposite direction for the other side of the winding. To tie off windings, use a modified rope "whipping" technique. As you near the end of the winding, lay a loop of monofilament fishing line along the top of the rod. Tape it in place if you have to. Continue wrapping over the fishing line. After about seven to ten turns, place the end of the wrapping through the end of the loop. Pull the loop back through the winding, pulling the end of the winding back underneath itself. Clip off the loose end with nail clippers.

Some rod winding thread is quite fuzzy. There are two ways of remedying this. You can use the blue flame from a gas stove to very lightly singe off the fuzz, or you can touch it with fine steel wool after it is sealed with finish. A good color preservative or fingernail polish should be applied to the windings before you apply a new coat of varnish. After the preservative is dry, put several good coats of rod covering or varnish over the windings to fill them up and smooth them out. Allow at least twenty-four hours drying time between coats. Lightly steel-wool the entire rod and apply a couple of coats of rod varnish to finish the rod.

REELS

At least once each year, tear down or "field strip" your fishing reel and completely clean it, replace any worn or broken parts and lubricate it according to your manufacturer's instructions. How far you tear it down depends on your tinkering ability, how bad shape it's in and whether or not you still have your owner's manual. The next time you buy a new reel, by all means file away the owner's manual in a safe place.

If you do any fishing at all, you're bound to run into a small problem sooner or later on your reel, even the best one made. Actually learning to tear your reel down on the kitchen table is great practice for that one time when they're "hittin' " and you've got a reel with a loose drag or a badly operating bail. It's great to be able to spot a minor problem, fix a loose nut or screw, or bend a washer a bit and not miss all the action. However, some fine reels are put together as precisely as a fine gun and do require patience in repair, so you must be your own judge as to where to stop in tearing down.

Cleaning and lubricating. Disassemble as far as you can and spray a good rust-inhibiting gun solvent into the inaccessible portions. Spray all accessible parts, wipe them clean and dry with a soft cloth. Lubricate according to your owner's manual. Usually one lubricates too much, yet not often enough. Lightly lubricate, then a month or so later, lightly lubricate again. Gear boxes of spinning reels should not be filled with grease. In fact, unless they have been broken or cracked to the point where water can get in, they're better off with the factory lubrication, even if it is discolored. However, if moisture has gotten in, carefully clean away the old grease and apply new. Use only an extremely lightweight grease such as is sold for

At end of season, a complete cleaning and lubricating will help prolong the life of your reel and improve its functioning.

reels or for lubricating power tools and fill the chamber about one-third full, making sure all contacting parts are completely submerged or covered with grease. A good adage in gunsmithing fits "reelsmithing" perfectly: Always use the correct size screwdriver. In other words do not use a screwdriver too large or too small for the screw, and you will have a better chance of removing the screw without damage to the reel.

Repairing reels.   Although dirt and abuse are the most common problems of all reels, each type has a particular problem or two of its own. One of the problems concerning the spincasting reel is that of catching a kink of line or foreign material between the revolving spool and the outer casing. This is remedied by slipping off the outer casing and removing the obstruction. A spincasting reel may fail to pick up line because of a weak line pick-up spring or a broken or worn pick-up pin. This means replacing that particular part. A problem with some spincasting reels is that the handle is a pressed-metal or cast affair and easily broken or bent. In many cases, you can replace it with a handle from a similar reel. This brings up a good point: Don't throw away old reels. Parts can often be interchanged. For instance, if you need a handle for a spinning reel, in many cases a handle from a similar reel can be made to fit with little effort. Usually, the reel fits over a half-round threaded shaft and is held in place by a locking nut.

One consistent problem with spinning reels, particularly with new line, is having the loop slip behind the spool and wind onto the shaft. If your reel is the "pop-on" type of spool, it's no problem. However, if your reel is not, you must first remove the drag setting knob, the drag washer (a small bent washer), a flat washer, a felt washer and finally the spool. One problem exclusive with spinning reels is the bail spring. This is a weak spot with many spinning reels. The only solution is to replace it. Not a complicated problem, but it does take about twelve fingers to hold everything in place while you replace the screws. With bait-casting reels, the main thing is to keep the revolving reel free of obstructions and well-lubricated to cut down on the possibility of birdsnests.

One of the problems with automatic fly reels is that the winding mechanism gets sprung or wound too tight. In this case, it's a matter of readjusting everything. Be careful in removing the case cover of a tightly "sprung" reel. The spring can pop out with a lot of force.

TACKLEBOXES

While you've got all the lures dumped out of your tacklebox, thoroughly clean it out with soap and water, rinse it and place it out in the sun to dry thoroughly. Rub a bit of petroleum jelly or gun lubricant on the hinges and locks. One good idea for protecting both tackebox and lures is to fit pieces of thin cork into the bottoms of the lure trays. This not only keeps the lures up out of the dampness that collects in the bottom of the trays, but prolongs the life of the tacklebox. To make your tacklebox quieter in a boat, apply cork to the bottom as well. Check handles frequently to make sure there are no cracks or areas that could break. Handles can be replaced with new ones of leather by using copper rivets. A good idea is to leave the box open for some time after each fishing trip to air it out and let the moisture evaporate.

Check hinges and fittings of tacklebox carefully. Lubricate with light machine or gun oil.

Steel tackleboxes can be rustproofed by spraying inside and out with a rust-inhibiting paint.

For protection of tacklebox, and to keep hooks of lures up out of dampness, line inside of trays with thin sheet of cork.

MISCELLANEOUS

For long life, cotton-twine landing nets can be occasionally treated with net preservative. Nylon nets do not require such treatment, and with proper care will last for many years. Any net should be hung up in a safe, dry area after use. Never leave folded or stored wet. Net repair kits also are available enabling the fisherman to replace any type of netting or twine at a nominal cost.

All metal fishing equipment, such as fish baskets, knives and aluminum tackleboxes, should be kept away from trolling motor batteries. If the battery acid is accidentally spilled, it can really make a mess out of metal equipment.

Naturally electronic gear, such as electronic fish finders, should be kept up out of the water. But if you drop one in the water, or it gets drenched in a thunderstorm, open it up and let it dry. If some of the connections are corroded with blue powder, swab them with cotton swabs and a bit of vinegar, then wash off the vinegar with water and cotton. Allow to dry thoroughly.

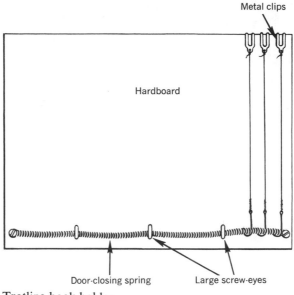

Trotline hook holder.

Styrofoam bait buckets and food coolers should be kept away from gasoline and gasoline fumes, as they have a tendency to eat into or soften the foam, as do many other solvents, including some of the bottled "pork" baits.

To keep the lids on your jars of pork baits from rusting shut, smear a bit of petroleum jelly around each rim.

All "trot-lines" and other lines with hooks on them should be strung on a container specifically made for the hooks and size of line. If you do very much trot-line or "limb-line" fishing, it's a good idea to have a separate tacklebox to hold all the large hooks and weights and balls of heavy string needed.

5 Boats and Canoes

All boats require maintenance. The amount of maintenance needed depends on the boat, what it's made of, where it's kept and how it is used. Regardless of what type, style, material, etc., a boat that gets normal usage should have at least a twice-yearly maintenance checkup. If you normally take your boat out of the water at the end of the fall season and store it for the winter, then this fall "laying up" is a familiar chore. However, many boat owners trailer their boats for each excursion, and this all-important chore sort of gets overlooked or forgotten.

FALL MAINTENANCE

In the fall is the time to do the majority of maintenance work, not in the spring when you're anxious to get on the water for a weekend of boating. Once your boat is out of the water, the first step is to wash and scrub any scum and fouling off the bottom of the hull. Do this while the boat is still wet, otherwise you'll end up using a heck of a lot of elbow grease to scrape and sand the fouling off. Clean the boat as thoroughly as possible, including carpeting, windshield, upholstery, etc. Use a good strong household cleaner to clean off any rubber trim such as around the windshield or the rub rail. Canvas boat tops should be washed with clean water, then given a good going over with canvas top cleaner. If the top is faded, spray on a light coat of canvas color renewer. Check the zippers of any side curtains and spray with a light gun-spray lubricant. Clean the plexiglass windshield using dish soap and water. If it is deeply scratched, use a windshield scratch-removing kit made for convertibles or boats.

For winter storage of your boat, make sure the upholstery is cleaned. If it is a bit shabby, renew it with a vinyl upholstery spray-on dye.

While you're cleaning, carefully check all fittings and replace or retighten any that are missing or loose. Inspect all rigging, etc. Remove any that you may wish to store ashore. Lightly sand and clean any varnish, retouching any that needs it. Touch up any paint or chipped spots using a matching color enamel or color-impregnated gel coat from your marine dealer. If your boat needs a complete paint job, now is the time to do it. Apply a good coat of boat wax to the outside surfaces. Flush out the bilge. Check the motor and battery, as covered in the next chapter. Some skippers like to turn their anchor ropes end-for-end each year to equalize the wear.

Open all lockers and leave open. Remove any items such as electronic gear, fishing, foodstuff, that might be stolen or that might spoil during storage. Open all vents. The boat should have plenty of ventilation during storage. Remove any cushions, sails, anchors or dock lines and allow them to air dry before storing.

The fall maintenance period is also the time to add any accessories you might want to make your boat more enjoyable.

Storing boats. A boat should be stored out of the weather if possible, and if this isn't possible, at least cover it completely.

Convertible boat tops should get the same treatment.

The interior of the boat can be freshened with a spray of speckle paint in a color to complement the exterior.

Rather than just throw a tarp over it, which will sag when filled with water and eventually leak, build a simple framework to support the canvas and keep it off the boat. Make sure you sponge up any water in the bilge. If you store your boat on a trailer with the trailer tongue lowered, first tip the tongue up and leave it for a bit with the boat drain open to allow any water to seep out. If your boat is fairly large, it should be supported on cradles or blocks to take some of the pressure off the trailer.

An excellent way of storing small car-top boats or canoes during off season is to hang them up in the top of the garage, just over the car. A system of pulleys and slings will make the job a snap. When you get ready to take off, position your car in place, lower the canoe or boat onto your car-top carrier and fasten in place. Unloading is as easy. Never store a canoe or similar boat lying right-side up on a garage floor. Sooner

Canoe can be stored in garage by hanging it from small pulleys or by laying it across rack hung from the ceiling.

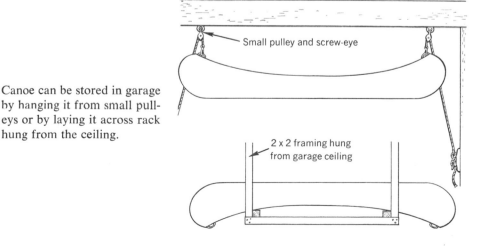

Small pulley and screw-eye

2 x 2 framing hung from garage ceiling

or later it will be filed with gear and junk, and if it's a canoe it will rock back and forth. This not only can cause damage to the frames, but a piece of gravel or debris under it can puncture or cause a bad dent.

Inflatable boats should be stored partially inflated in a cool dry spot. Rubber surfaces can be lightly dusted with talcum powder for extra protection.

ALUMINUM BOATS

In theory, aluminum boats are the easiest to maintain. Although aluminum dents easily, it stretches and you will normally have few holes to patch, although several dents. The dents can usually be smoothed out with a rubber mallet, holding a block of wood as an "anvil" against the opposite side. The best method is that used by an automobile body and fender repairman. He doesn't hit the dent head in the center, but starts on the outside circumference and works in. If the metal has been stretched too far, as in a deep dent, and may possibly rupture, drill a small hole in the deepest part of the dent before pounding it back in place.

With the dent hammered back in place, sand the area thoroughly with No. 120 wet-or-dry sandpaper and fill it with a plastic body putty such as used by auto-body mechanics. After the compound has set up, sand the area using an orbital sander on an electric drill. Touch up any missing paint. Make sure you use an aluminum primer before applying the paint.

Repairing holes and cracks.   A small hole in aluminum can usually be patched with a bit of plastic metal applied to the outside surface of the boat. The surface must be absolutely dry, which usually is no problem if you can get the damaged area above water line. The metal will dry quickly in the sun. A rivet can be used to stop up a small hole. However, larger holes will require a patch riveted on the outside of the hole. The first step is to smooth the entire area down to the bare metal with steel wool. Then cut a patch of the size to fit the damage. Drill matching holes in both the boat and the patch. Coat the patch and the area with either plastic aluminum or a

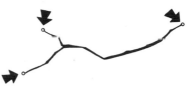

If a crack develops, drill small holes at each end before patching.

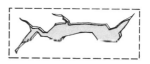

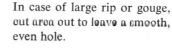

In case of large rip or gouge, cut area out to leave a smooth, even hole.

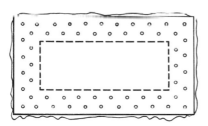

Cut a patch about 2 inches larger than the cutout, cover back with plastic aluminum. Drill two rows of holes and hammer in place.

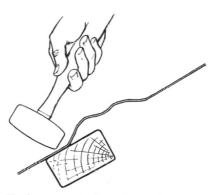

To hammer back a dent, always start on outside edge, work towards center.

good two-part epoxy glue, press in position and rivet in place. Make sure you have enough plastic aluminum or epoxy smeared between to seal the rivet holes. When the patch has set and hardened, use a file to smooth down the squeezed out plastic or epoxy.

If a crack has developed, before you can patch it you should drill a small hole at each end to prevent it from cracking further. Most repairs on aluminum boats will be by riveting, and you should occasionally examine your boat and retighten any loose rivets. This is an easy job with two people, one to hold an anvil or heavy metal hammer or object on the inside of the boat while the other whacks the outside ends of the rivets with a ball peen hammer. Any time you replace rivets they must be dipped into an anticorrosive liquid such as zinc chromate before inserting in their holes.

Any fittings other than aluminum, particularly those containing bronze, copper or brass, that are fastened to an aluminum boat will cause galvanic action and corrosion problems. A rubber or cork gasket must be used between these fittings and an aluminum hull.

Miscellaneous care.   If you have an aluminum boat which is used extensively in salt water, it should be hosed off with fresh water after each use. To get an aluminum boat really clean, scrub it with a mild solution of TSP (trisodium phosphate) and soapy water, then hose it off good with fresh water. Make sure you remove all the TSP, or it will continue working. Or you can use an abrasive cleaner made especially for brightening aluminum.

An aluminum boat must be prepared carefully for a good paint job. Check with your manufacturer for the correct paints, primers, etc. The first step in painting is to clean the boat thoroughly as mentioned above, removing all scum, fouling and salts. For a good-bonding paint job, you must give the boat a coat of thinned primer. Follow this with at least two coats of primer, then apply a coat of the recommended marine paint. If you use copper antifouling paints, a coat of zinc chromate must be used as a primer.

WOODEN BOATS

Practically all of the problems that trouble wooden boats can be traced to rot or its resulting damages.The old-timers knew that rot was an enemy to fight constantly both with prevention and repair. If wood is kept at a constant and fairly dry moisture content it won't rot, but the only sure way you could guarantee the wood in your boat wouldn't rot would be to put it in a bottle. There are, however, several things you can do to protect your boat and prevent it from rotting as quickly.

Protecting against rot. Rot is worst in any hard-to-get-to spot in the boat that collects and holds moisture or water. Allow sufficient drainage and ventilation in all areas of this nature. This may require installing several new drains or vents, but if it saves you having to replace planking or decking, it's worth it.

Linseed oil applied boiling hot (always use a double boiler for this, because the oil is flammable) and liberally, will do a lot toward preventing rot. You can also use penetrating oils, such as used for refinishing furniture. However, they are quite a bit more expensive than linseed oil.

Any rotting members should be replaced as soon as they're discovered. A broken or cracked frame, or even a canoe rib, can sometimes be replaced, but it's usually easier to "scab" a duplicate to the original. If you need to laminate strips together for fastening to a frame member, or for building a new one, use epoxy or resorcinol glue and clamp the members with rubber-band clamps. If you use plywood in repairing a boat it must be marine grade, not exterior or the so-called waterproof plywood.

Dry rot is actually one of the worst offenders, and it really isn't rot, but deterioration of the wood caused by a fungus growth. However, the fungus growth starts only in damp, unventilated areas, and usually these are hard-to-see and get-at corners. The spores attach to the wood, leaving nothing but a powdery mass, and like any other fungus will spread if not stopped. The best preventive for dry rot is plenty of ven-

Rot, the enemy of wooden boats, must be fought constantly.

tilation, particularly in boat bottoms, under decks, etc. The fungus also cannot live in an area that is occasionally washed with salt water. In fact, many fresh-water boaters wash out the bilge occasionally with salt water just to stop the possibility of dry rot in those areas.

Fiberglassing boats. Whether to fiberglass or not is one question almost any wooden boat owner asks himself at one time or another. Unfortunately many people think they can cover the exterior hull of a wooden boat no matter what shape it's in with a coating of fiberglass and the boat will last as long as a fiberglass boat, and with the same minimum amount of maintenance. This just isn't so. Moisture collects on the inside of the boat from condensation, rainwater, spray and wet people and because the water can't work its way back through because of the fiberglass covering, it may cause rotting of the important structural members as bad or worse in some areas than if the boat never had been fiberglassed. The argu-

82

ment for fiberglassing, and a very good one, is that it provides strength on impact.

A similar problem may develop if the exterior shell of fiberglass over the wood has a flaw in it, allowing moisture to seep in. Again the main problem is getting rid of the moisture. If you fiberglass a wooden boat, it must be done properly and following the instructions of the resin manufacturer carefully, according to mix, timing, temperatures. You must also provide adequate ventilation under the boat decks, in addition to good drainage in the bottom of the boat. All paint, dirt, scum, etc., must be removed before applying the fiberglass coating. Do not use a blow torch to remove the paint, as you run the risk of driving some of the melted paint into the wood pores. Use a scraper, chemical stripper and belt or orbital sander. The sandpaper should be a coarse, open-coat paper to roughen the wood and give the fiberglass coat good adhesion. Fill the cracks or seams in the wood, using a mixture of ground fiberglass fibers and resin, or you can substitute resin and talcum powder. Fill all cracks and sand smooth. This type of caulking will adhere to the final coat of fiberglass, whereas caulking compounds containing oil or tar will not. By the same token, don't use gasoline to clean the wood. Fiberglass will not adhere properly if there are any traces of petroleum products in the wood.

Cut the fiberglass cloth to fit the general hull shape. Always cut the cloth with scissors, not a knife. Make sure you have plenty of cloth. If your boat is large, you will probably have to cover only one side or a section of a hull at a time. After cutting the cloth, roll it around a broom handle or long dowel. Mix the resin and catalyst as per the instructions, adding coloring agent if called for. Watch your working time, noting the temperature you're working in and the amount of catalyst added to the resin. Working as quickly as possible, paint on a full wet coat of resin, using a roller or paint brush. Watch the wood and if any areas appear dull, apply more resin. As soon as you've quickly covered the boat, put down the cloth. This is where the dowel comes in handy; you can roll down the cloth quickly and without wrinkles. Nothing beats your fingers for

To fiberglass a boat, mix the resin and catalyst as per the manufacturer's instructions.

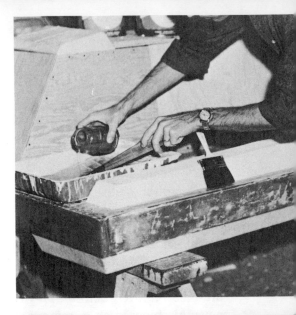

Paint the resin on in a full coat, then lay the fiberglass cloth in position. Smooth it down with your fingers, making sure all bubbles are out.

With the cloth in place, brush on another coat of resin, allow it to dry, sand lightly with medium paper No. 80 and apply a final, full coat.

working the cloth down into the resin and smoothing it out, but make sure you have the proper cleaner. When you have the cloth as smooth as possible, go to the next area. Overlap at least 2 to 6 inches and continue until the entire boat is covered. Then apply a new coat of resin with coloring agent in a full wet coat to the entire boat.

Allow the coating to harden overnight, then using a sharp knife, belt sander or rasp, trim off the rough edges. Lightly sand the entire boat and apply a final coat. When this is dry give it a good coating of wax, mount your hardware back in place and you're ready to go.

Sealing boats.   Actually the best thing you can do with most wooden boats, particularly those that stay in the water, is to seal them properly, then apply the proper paint or varnish. And that's where modern technology really combines with age-old techniques. Today's new synthetic-rubber and silicone sealers and caulking compounds are far ahead of yesterday's old caulking materials both in performance and application. But many of the rules for applying have not changed in a hundred years. In applying any caulking or sealer make sure that you completely fill the area you are caulking, or again you defeat yourself. When the moisture comes in through a tiny opening it cannot get out through the caulking compound, so it soaks into the wood.

Any seams in wooden boats should be carefully checked and caulked prior to repainting. Scarf-joint seams on plywood boats are usually the hardest to patch properly.

Painting and varnishing boats. The first step in applying a good protective paint or varnish surface to a boat is to pull it out of the water and clean it as thoroughly as possible. The old paint should be removed using a good-quality water-wash stripper. This is painted on in a heavy coat, allowed to "work," then hosed off with water. If there is more than one coat of paint, which there normally is, the hosed-off boat should be allowed to dry, then another coat of stripper painted on. This again is allowed to work, then using water and coarse steel wool, the softened paint is scrubbed off. This is much easier than using scrapers. However a canvas surface must be carefully scraped, rather than stripped, as you might loosen the canvas with the stripper.

For a good high-gloss paint job the surface of the boat must be prepared correctly. Use a liquid filler to fill the open pores of the wood. This is especially important on oak. All nail holes should be filled. Sand the wooden surface as smooth as possible and apply a metallic primer. After forty-eight hours of drying in normal temperatures and humidity (this is one project for the shade), sand the first coat down to the bare wood using a hand sander and wet-or-dry sandpaper No. 220. Apply a couple of coats of waterproof undercoat, again sanding between each coat with wet-or-dry sandpaper in the same grit. Finally, apply at least five coats of high-gloss marine finish. This should be sprayed on if possible, and should be sanded between coats with silicone carbide wet-or-dry finishing paper No. 600. The paint should be thinned according to the manufacturer's instructions to achieve the optimum gloss. The final step is to apply a good marine wax.

Before repainting, a wooden boat must be stripped down to the bare wood using chemical strippers and power sanders. An open-coat, non-clogging sandpaper must be used in power sander.

Varnishing is much the same, except you must be much more careful in preparing the surface. The main problem in varnishing, one that causes furniture manufacturers fits, is to get all the sanding dust and grit off the surface before you apply the varnish. You should vacuum the surface if possible. Then wipe down the entire area with a tack cloth. Apply the first coat of varnish, thinned about one-third with turpentine. Apply another coat and sand down to the bare wood with wet-or-dry sandpaper No. 220. Apply another coat, this time full-strength, and sand only until smooth. Apply at least three more coats, sanding between each with silicone carbide wet-or-dry sandpaper No. 400.

A boat covered with a high-gloss paint or varnish should never be washed with anything but soft soap such as dish soap and warm water.

FIBERGLASS BOATS

Contrary to popular belief, fiberglass boats are not maintenance free. The exterior gel coat will eventually deteriorate, may need to be patched and eventually may need to be painted. Once it has been painted, you have a surface that continually needs maintenance, much the same as a wooden boat. However, fiberglass will normally require the least amount of maintenance and care. Light scratches can usually be removed using water and ordinary sink cleaner. Warm soapy water will remove most other material. TSP will remove any stubborn stains, but will also leave the surface somewhat dulled.

Fiberglass boats actually require the least amount of maintenance when new.

Nicks and scratches in a fiberglass boat can easily be repaired using a kit made for patching fiberglass gel-coats.

Bolts and plastic washers

Three methods of fastening fittings to fiberglass boats.

Wooden plate to fit inside of hull

Sheet-metal screws, ends covered with globs of epoxy glue

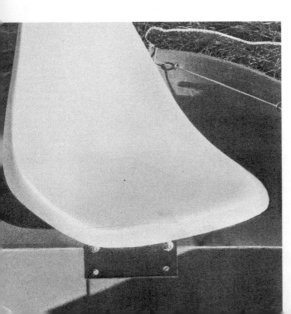

Fiberglass bucket seats are popular in today's modern fishing boats. When attaching, bed the bolts or screws in epoxy cement for a stronger, longer-lasting mount.

Oarlocks should occasionally be dusted with a light lubricant to prevent them from squeaking, an annoyance to any duck hunter.

Clamp-on running lights are also becoming popular as more and more small boats take to the large lakes. A tiny hole drilled in their bottom will allow rain water and spray to seep out.

A battery used in a small boat should always be clamped down or have a definite spot where it can't easily be tipped over and spill the battery acid onto the boat floor.

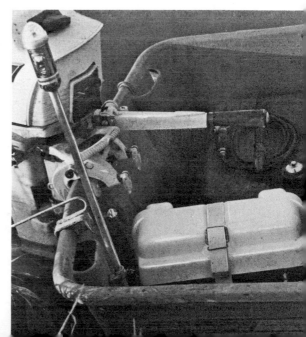

When mounting accessories on small fiberglass boats, use epoxy as a bedding compound to provide more strength and a better fit.

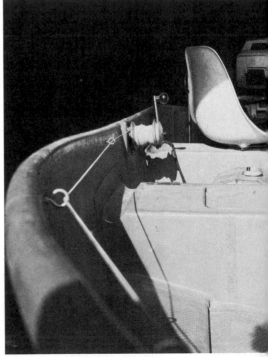

A cockpit anchor crank is a joy to any angler. The anchor line should be threaded through guides to the front of the boat. Guides are screweyes bolted in place with plastic washers.

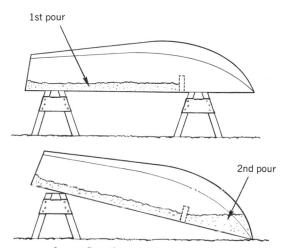

1st pour

2nd pour

Places to pour foam flotation. First pour is under gunwales to bulkhead. Second pour is at bow. A third pour can be made under floorboards.

For additional flotation, foam plastic can be sprayed on the underside of boat or side decks with the boat inverted.

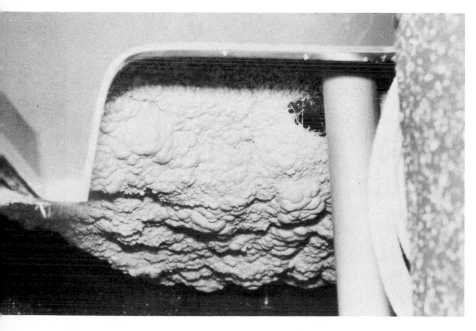

Every boat boat powered with a gasoline engine should have a good fire extinguisher.

A damaged area on a fiberglass boat can usually be patched using a two-part epoxy filler, or fiberglass patches and matching resin. In patching with fiberglass, the surface must be absolutely dry, free of powder, dust or oil. All paint and stripper must be removed and the fiberglass sanded down to a clean surface.

CANVAS CANOES

Small holes in canvas canoes can be patched with chewing gum, plain old pine gum or black plastic electrician's tape. If you use pine gum, heat it a bit and mix in a bit of bacon fat.

Carry a roll of copper wire on a canoe trip and use it to lace up any broken ribs or frames. A rawhide lacing applied wet and allowed to dry will work as well, as will a lacing cut from wild cherry root-bark.

A cracked canoe paddle can be reglued using epoxy glue. The paddle can be clamped with a section of rubber-band clamp cut from an old inner tube. The insides and duckboards of canoes should be painted in a flat glare-free paint such as duck-boat paint. This is not only cooler, but less slippery when wet.

A large hole or gouge in a canvas and wood canoe can be patched with a piece of canvas and household cement or canvas cement. The patch should be coated thoroughly with cement and a thin layer spread around the torn area. Place the patch in position, tape it down with electrician's tape and allow it to dry for an hour. When you get home, sand the rough edges down to blend in with the surrounding surface.

Canvas, or canvas and fiberglass, canoes can be patched in camp using chewing gum, melted pine pitch, or plastic electricians tape.

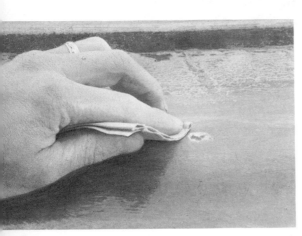

First step in an at-home canoe repair is sanding the damaged area with medium No. 80 sandpaper.

Coat the area liberally with a mix of fiberglass resin and catalyst.

Place a fiberglass cloth patch over the area, press out all the bubbles and smooth down the cloth. Paint on a full wet coat of resin and leave for twenty-four hours, then sand with fine No. 400 sandpaper.

The interior of a canoe and duck-boards should be painted with a good, flat marine paint such as that used for painting duck boats.

A cracked canoe paddle can sometimes be patched using epoxy glue and held in place with clamps cut from an inner tube until glue sets.

Some canoeists, especially canoe anglers, like to tie their canoe paddles to the canoe. When they get a fish on, they can quickly drop their paddle without having to lay it in the canoe.

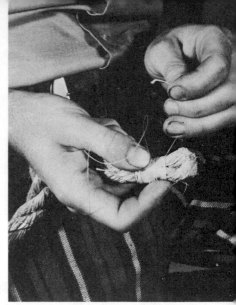

Sails made of synthetic materials are the easiest to care for. Should occasionally be scrubbed with soapy water, then rinsed and allowed to air dry.

The end of a cotton or manila rope will last much longer if it is whipped. The easy way of whipping is to lay a loop of fishing line under the last few turns. Then thread the end of the whipping thread through the fishing line and pull the thread back under itself.

SAILS

Canvas sails require hosing off with fresh water after use in salt water. Always stow canvas sails dry, or they will mildew or rot. Synthetic sails require less attention. However, all sails should occasionally be washed in soapy water, using a light scrub brush. Then air dry them thoroughly before storing. Sails may be darned using the automatic stitching awl or by hand and using a palm. '

ROPES

Ropes should always be stored in a well-ventilated area and loosely coiled so they will not rot. Frequently check rigging and replace or repair any that needs it.

SPRING MAINTENANCE

If you did your work properly in the fall, about all that needs to be done in the spring is to check to make sure all equipment is functioning, then head for the water.

6 Outboard Motors

In the "olden" days, an outboard was a cranky, oil-spewing, hard-to-start but necessary piece of equipment for the serious fisherman or outdoorsman. Today's easy-starting, smooth-running, powerful motors are an altogether different story. However, their theory of operation is the same regardless of the refinements, and even today's outboards require a regular "schedule" of care and maintenance. This maintenance can be broken down into three periods: preseason, postseason storage and during the season. If your motor was properly maintained for the postseason storage, you could probably get by with little except refueling, wiping off the dust and cranking. However, by following a good preseason schedule, you can insure your motor will crank over the first time.

GENERAL MAINTENANCE

Most outboards are two-cycle engines and their fuel must be mixed with oil for internal lubrication. All outboards do not require the same ratio of fuel and oil. Determine the correct fuel-oil ratio mix from your manual, write it in waterproof ink on a piece of tape and apply this to your gas tank, and you'll always have the correct fuel-mix ratio with you. On some motors, the fuel-oil ratio is stated inside the top cover of the motor. An outboard will run on a wrong fuel-oil ratio, or poorly mixed fuel oil; however, it's not only hard on the motor but you will constantly be adjusting the carburetor and choke adjustments just to keep your motor operating. The fuel used should be a marine white gas or a good-quality regular gas. The oil mixed with it should be an outboard motor oil if available. Or use a regular-grade automotive oil. Do not use one of the high-priced premium oils with additives. They may

Mix outboard fuel and oil in a separate container from the gas tank to the exact ratio of oil and fuel as specified in your owner's manual. Shake it well before pouring into the gas tank.

be fine for your car but can really wreak havoc on a two-cycle engine. Always mix the fuel and oil in a container large enough to hold both the required amounts of fuel and oil for your specific ratio. The container should be a separate one from the fuel tank. To get a thoroughly mixed fuel, pour in a little fuel, the required oil, and thoroughly shake, then add the remaining gasoline. When pouring the gas and oil into the tank, always use a funnel with a filter. If you fill your remote tank at service stations, it's a good idea to take along a good marine funnel. This has an extremely fine screen and will catch water droplets as well as particles of dirt and lint.

When starting your outboard, pull out the starter cord firmly and swiftly, then let it rewind slowly. Do not let it snap back, as you run the risk of breaking the cord or snapping the starter rewind spring. Each time you start your motor, make it a habit to check the discharge. If your engine does not have a thermo-

Frequently check the water discharge tube, particularly if you're running in weedy or mossy water. The tube must be discharging coolant at all times.

stat, it should start spitting water out of the discharge tube immediately. However, if your motor is equipped with a thermostat, it may take a few minutes of warming up before it opens up. If there is no water spurting out of the discharge tube, take your motor to your dealer for a new water pump or to check the thermostat. Make sure it is discharging coolant at all times. This is especially important if you're running in shallow or mossy water, so keep a good watch on the discharge.

Always carry a pair of pliers, a screwdriver, a spark plug wrench, a pair of properly gapped spark plugs, extra shear pins and cotter keys, and if your prop has one, a rubber-cushioning block stowed away in a safe place in your boat.

The following maintenance suggestions apply to outboards in general; you will have to follow your owner's manual for specific information. You will also have to be your own judge as to what problems to tackle and what to take to your dealer.

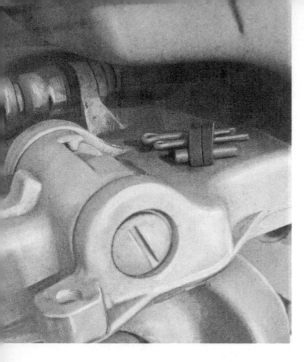

If your motor doesn't have spare shear pins and cotter keys attached as this one does, carry a couple of spares in your tacklebox or boat storage compartment.

PRESEASON CARE

Remove any dust cover you may have thrown over the stored outboard. Remove the motor-housing cover, pull the starter cord out slowly to its full length and examine it for frayed or cut portions. If the cord is extremely bad, replace it. Don't take a chance on being caught out with a broken starter rope. Although replacing a starter rope is not a complicated problem, you will need to refer to the exploded drawing or parts list in your owner's manual for specific information. However, be careful of the recoil spring; it can unwind suddenly when removed, causing injury. If your starter clatters, check the flywheel. If it is loose, tighten using the proper wrench.

Checking spark plugs.   Remove the spark plugs and inspect them. If your plugs look pretty good, clean them with a fine emery cloth, gap them to the proper specifications as per your owner's manual and replace. If the plugs need replacement, examine them and note their exact condition. The condition of the plugs indicates whether your motor is operating properly or not, and if not, where the problem is. A plug operating normally should have a light gray or tan insulator tip. There should be little or no combustion deposits on the tip. If the plugs have burned electrodes, this usually means the carburetor setting is too lean, there is an air leak in the fuel line from the tank to the fuel pump or there is a loose carburetor mounting. A plug with bridged-over or shorted-out electrodes means excessive carbon in the cylinder, caused by improper fuel-oil mixture. If the spark plug tips are black and damp with oil film, it means excessive oil in the fuel, the idle speed may be too low, the idle adjustment too rich. Replace the defective plugs with the plugs specified in your owner's manual, properly gapped. Check the plug cords and the insulating rubber surrounding them for any breaks or deterioration.

A quick test for ignition problems is to remove one of the spark plugs, ground it against the motor housing and with the end about 1/16-inch away from the motor housing turn the motor over using the starter cord. If the spark jumping across is a blue color, you have no problems. However, if you get no spark or the spark is a weak yellow color, take your motor to your dealer for ignition servicing before the season starts.

If your motor is an electric start, examine the starter and battery leads for any breaks or deterioration. Remove the battery connections and clean them and the battery terminals. The battery can be cleaned with a solution of baking soda and water. Replace and coat with a good coating of grease to prevent corrosion. Make sure the battery is fully charged.

Checking the fuel system. A quick check of your fuel system is to connect the fuel tank, remove carburetor's lowest drain screw, then pump priming bulb. If a steady flow of gas runs from the hole, the fuel system is O.K. If there is no fuel or erratic spurts coming from the drain hole, remove the fuel before it reaches the carburetor. If fuel spurts out, you have blockage in the carburetor, and should have a carburetor overhaul. If there is no fuel coming from fuel line, the problem is in either the tank or fuel line. Examine the fuel lines from the fuel intake to the carburetor. Replace any fuel lines that are deteriorated or flattened, indicating weak spots. If the motor is very old, it's a good idea to replace the fuel lines completely. This is a matter of cutting the rubber hose to length, slipping the new lines over the nipples and shoving the circle clamps in place. Check the fuel filter bowl, drain and clean it, replace the filter if it is damaged or too badly clogged.

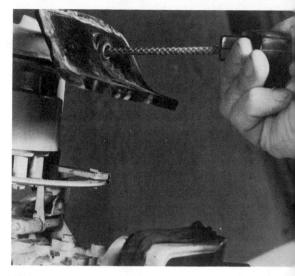

1. First step in checking over your outboard before starting a season of boating is to pull the starter rope out slowly and examine carefully for abrasions or breaks. Replace if there are any bad spots.

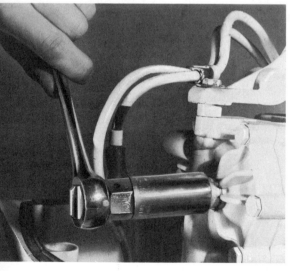

2. Remove the spark plugs using a good plug wrench and inspect them carefully. The condition of your plugs will indicate any problems you may have with the motor.

3. Inspect and flex the plug wires. If any are brittle or you suspect a break, replace them with new ones.

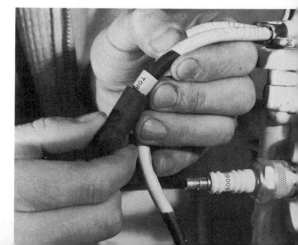

4. Using a solution of baking soda and water, clean the battery and connections. Use sandpaper to brighten the terminals. Flush the exterior of the battery with fresh water. Fill the cells with rainwater or distilled water and recharge using a slow charge.

5. Check the fuel filter bowl, clean it, replace the filter if it is damaged or badly clogged.

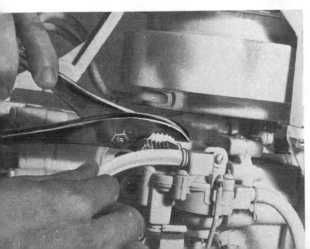

6. Inspect the fuel lines and replace any that may have tiny cracks or deteriorating connections.

7. One of the most common problems with remote fuel tanks is a broken or chipped O-ring inside the connector. A quick inspection of this tiny rubber ring can save a frustrating "no-start" trip.

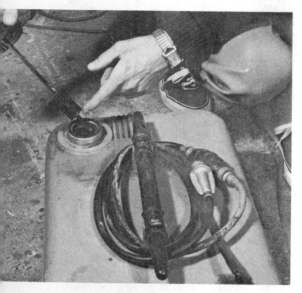

8. This is also a good time to examine your fuel level indicator in the fuel tank.

9. Always check and grease the swivel pins before each season. On most outboards, a grease fitting will be installed on both top and bottom pins. On some outboards there will also be a grease fitting for the shift lever.

If you have a remote fuel tank, check the hose and fittings for loose connections, or a broken or collapsed hose. Also examine the tiny O-ring inside the fuel connector. If it is smashed or chipped, replace it. This is a common problem causing your fuel pump to suck air, and create a hard-to-start or poorly running engine.

Also check the gasket in the filler cap and the pick-up filter in your gas tank. To check this filter, you will have to remove the fuel-line connector from the tank. The filter is attached to the end of the draw tube.

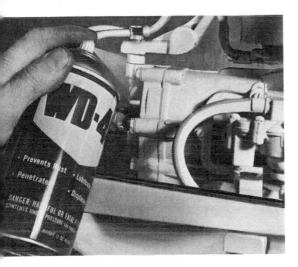

Light dusting coat of penetrating moisture-displacing oil will protect your outboard's electrical system from the weather and constant moisture problems.

Checking the grease fittings.   On some outboards, you will find standard grease fittings on the upper and lower swivel pins, as well as for the gear-shift lever. Lubricate these with a good-quality grease from a grease gun or tube. If your outboard does not have a fitting you will have to work a bit of grease in around the swivel pin by hand.

Checking the linkages.   Check all the mechanical linkages inside the motor housing and tighten all the screws and bolts. Replace any that are missing. Place a few drops of lightweight motor oil on all the connecting linkages such as carburetor, steering, speed control, etc.

To drain the lubricant from the lower end, check your owner's manual for the proper position of the outboard. Some outboards drain best in a horizontal position, some in a vertical. Vent plug as well as drain plug must be removed.

Replacing the lubricant. Drain the lubricant from the lower unit. To do this, remove both the oil-drain and vent screws as per your owner's manual. Most motors will have to be in a vertical position to drain fully. Refill the lower unit with the proper outboard gear lubricant until it flows out the vent plug, or as specified in your owner's manual. Check the gaskets on both screws and replace if they're bad. Poorly fitting or worn gaskets enable air and water to get into the unit, shortening the life of your motor.

Replace vent plug and refill lower end with lower-end lubricant as specified in your owner's manual. Make sure the gaskets on both screws haven't worn out.

Checking the propeller.   Remove the propeller and check for any fishing line that may have wound onto the shaft. It's unbelievable the amount of line that can get wound onto your propeller shaft and go unnoticed. Check the shear pin and replace it if it is bent or cracked. Coat the propeller shaft lightly with grease or vasoline. Examine the propeller for nicks or dents. You can file out small nicks with a good bastard mill file. However, if a chunk of the propeller is missing, it could throw the propeller out of balance, so replace it with a new one. If your motor has a rubber-cushioning block, position it over the shear pin, then place the propeller over the rubber block, making sure the protrusion in the end of the prop fits into the front slot of the rubber block. Replace the washer, turn the nut on by hand, then tighten it a half-turn or until the slots line up, enabling you to replace the cotter key.

Few sportsmen realize the problems they cause when they strip a birdsnest from a reel, cut it off and throw it overboard. This monofilament line had eventually worked itself behind the rubber cushioning block until it had fractured the block.

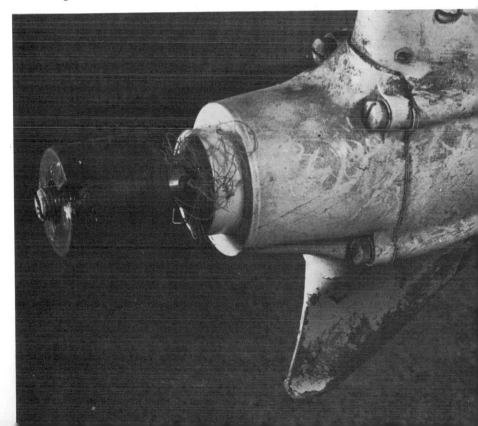

Checking the motor.   Wipe all of the dust and dirt out of your motor and touch up any chipped paint spots with a bit of touch-up paint. This little chore not only gives you a better-looking motor but the minute inspection enables you to spot a small problem before it becomes a big headache.

If you stored your motor on your boat, check to make sure the transom screws are tight. However, don't force them, tighten them only with your hands. It's a good idea to use a safety chain or cable to fasten the outboard to your boat, as a friend of mine recently found out. Cruising in the shallow arm of an unfamiliar lake, he hit a stump with his outboard. It popped off and sank in about five feet of water. He quickly retrieved it, rowed back to the dock, went home and immediately tore the motor down. He took the cover off, took the wires loose from the spark plugs, removed the spark plugs and sprayed diaelectric rust preventive into the cylinders and every other spot he could inject the tiny nozzle into. He removed the carburetor cover, took off all fuel lines and allowed everything to dry thoroughly. A couple of days later he lubricated the motor in every way he could think of, put it back together, took it back to the dock and the seven-year-old motor fired after the third try. Needless to say, he has taken a lot of kidding, but he now has two transom cables attached to his motor.

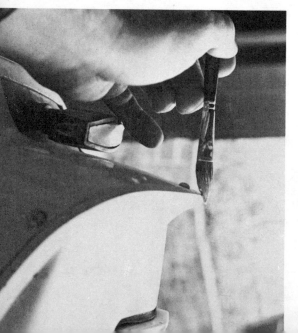

Any chipped spots of paint can be retouched with lacquer normally used for plastic models, blended to match the paint on your outboard. Some of the newer outboards also have paints that practically match the touch-up sprays for automobiles.

Before starting each season, and before each trip, check the transom screws. They should be hand tight.

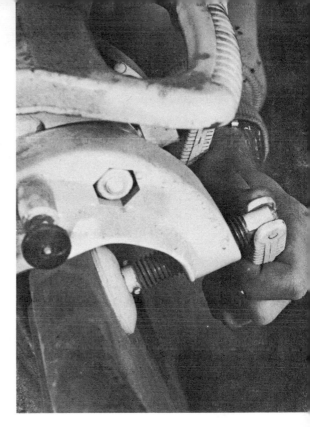

Wiping your motor clean with a cloth lightly soaked in oil not only makes your motor appear better, but gives you a good chance to examine it carefully while you work.

109

Things to watch for. If you followed the preseason in-spection and maintenance, you should have no problem start-ing your outboard. However, if you do, the following causes could give you an indication where the trouble might be.

1. Empty fuel tank—don't laugh, it's happened.
2. Motor-speed control not positioned on start—very im-portant on some motors to keep from flooding.
3. Motor not choked to start.
4. Engine not primed—squeeze bulb on tank should pump till firm.
5. Water in fuel tank.
6. Fuel not getting to carburetor. Check area of fuel stop-page by removing the high-speed adjusting screw. If fuel runs out, look back to fuel tank or connecting line. Problem could be dirty filter in fuel tank pickup, kink in fuel line, faulty O-ring, or even as simple as the tank not being vented. Air vent on tank must be open.
7. Carburetor adjustments too lean—turn slightly coun-terclockwise.
8. Carburetor float sticking—tap on carburetor.
9. Crankcase flooded—remove spark plugs, dry off mois-ture, turn flywheel several times to dry out crankcase, replace spark plugs.
10. Spark plugs or ignition faulty—check by removing plug, grounding end and turning over motor. Bright blue spark indicates healthy ignition.

DURING-SEASON CARE

Periodic maintenance during the season will greatly help extend your outboard's life and make it operate more smoothly. If your motor is used in salt water, flush it out with fresh water by attaching a hose to the water intake. You will need a spe-cial hose-attachment jig available from your marine dealer for most outboards. Use only a moderate amount of water pres-sure, or you may damage the water-intake impeller. You should also hose down the outside of your motor each time you remove it from the water. Follow this with a thorough wiping down with a soft, lightly oiled rag. When you're through using the motor for the day or weekend, be sure and remove the fuel-tank line and run the motor to draw the fuel out of the fuel lines and carburetor before pulling the motor out of the water for travel or storage. This is an especially important rule during cold weather use such as by duck hunters and cold-weather fishermen.

Occasionally give the motor a good polishing with automobile wax. If you store your motor outside, or trailer it to those favorite fishing spots, use a motor cover to keep out dust and rainwater. If your motor is carried in the back of your

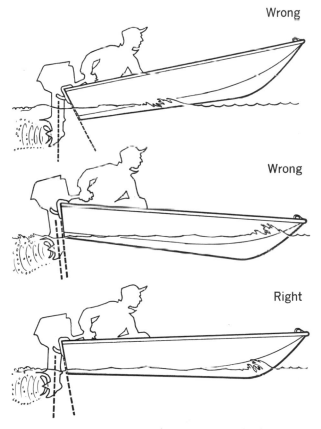

Correct motor angle makes running easier on both boat and motor, is safer, uses less fuel.

Anytime you tilt a small outboard, grasp it at the top rear of the case to pull forward rather than pushing down on the handle. You run the risk of damaging the controls if you strain the handle.

car or station wagon, use a plastic or cloth bag to protect it from dust and grit. It should also be tied down to keep from bouncing around. Whenever you tilt a lightweight motor, grasp it by the rear of the motor housing. Do not tilt it by pushing down on the steering handle. One rule sometimes learned the hard way is that most outboards will not go into reverse with their motors choked, so don't try to force your motor into reverse gear immediately after starting it, if you've still got it choked.

After a couple of months of operation, you should give your motor another maintenance job.

1. Drain the gearcase of lower unit and refill with correct lubricant.
2. Remove the fuel bowl and clean bowl and filter. Replace filter if necessary.

3. Inspect, clean and regap spark plugs.
4. Check propeller for chips or cracks.
5. Inspect shear pin or rubber cushioning block and replace if damaged.
6. Lubricate all grease fittings, particularly those pertaining to the swivel pin.
7. Inspect and lightly oil all remote controls, linkages, etc.
8. If your motor is an electric start, clean and coat the battery terminals with grease.
9. Check water pump.

POSTSEASON STORAGE

Drain the carburetor float chamber and remove the fuel filter bowl. Clean and replace the filter element and the gasket. Drain the fuel tank and clean it to remove any accumulated varnish and gum. The easiest method for doing this is to place a bit of lacquer thinner and pebbles in the tank, rinse it with clean gasoline and allow it to dry thoroughly before replacing the cap. (Do this entire operation outdoors.)

Drain the gearcase and refill with the correct lubricant. Spray a light coat of rust preventive around the powerhead. Disconnect the spark plug leads, remove the spark plugs and place about a teaspoon of light oil into the ports and crank the motor a few times to lubricate the cylinders. Leave the plug leads off to prevent someone accidentally starting the motor. Wipe over the entire motor with a cloth lightly soaked in oil. Either store the motor in a standing position in an out-of-the way place of your garage or leave it on your boat. Cover it with a cloth to keep off dust and debris.

Repairing trolling motors. Trolling motors normally require very little maintenance. However, when they do break down they can usually be repaired quite easily. No matter how big and "gadgety" they are, they're basically just a small electric motor running from a 6- to 12-volt battery.

If your motor bogs down the first thing to do is to check the propeller for tangled fishing line or moss. If the motor continues to hum or bog down, check for battery charge. If the

Electric trolling motors, particularly foot-operated front motors, have been the boon of the serious fisherman. They are one of the most efficient pieces of equipment you can have.

The main problem with foot-operated controls for electric motors is keeping the electrical connections from getting wet. This is almost impossible when you get in rough weather and take on a bit of water. When this happens, remove the cover as soon as possible and allow the connections to dry thoroughly.

A moisture-displacing lubricating spray will help keep your trolling motor controls operating properly.

battery is properly charged, the seal on the lower unit may be broken and water may be in motor. If your motor is still under warranty, working on the lower unit will normally void the warranty on it. However, if the motor is past the warranty stage, you can usually find the problem easily yourself. Remove the motor from the housing and examine for any water damage. When replacing, you may need new O-rings to achieve a proper seal.

If the motor stops dead or refuses to turn over, start at the off-and-on switch and examine each wire and electrical connection. Using a simple homemade tester you can check for voltage starting at the switch and going to the motor terminals to determine exactly where the problem is. If the trolling motor is complicated with a rheostat or foot-operated controls, you have even more steps that can be causing the trouble. Each connection should be checked in the order that the current flows from the battery.

If a trolling motor is left on a boat while the boat is being transported, the vibration can loosen several parts. Occasionally check all screws and allen screws and retighten or replace any that are missing. If the motor is used in salt water, it should be thoroughly washed down after each trip.

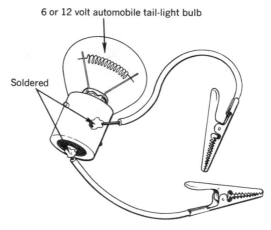

6 or 12 volt automobile tail-light bulb

Soldered

Voltage tester for checking a
trolling motor.

One of the greatest products fishermen have discovered is the foot-operated controls for trolling motors. However, they do have one drawback. These foot controls are usually located near the bottom of the boat and in a rainstorm or rough water, the foot controls get flooded. Normally all that is needed is to remove all plates, brush the corrosion off the electrical connections and allow the entire unit to dry out. Spraying with dialectric-spray, (a "drying-out" protective agent) will help in future dunkings.

7 Boating and Camping Trailers

Nothing can wreck a fishing or camping trip as quickly as highway trailer trouble. A burned-out wheel bearing or flat tire can mean delays that may make the difference in a successful or unsuccessful hunting or fishing trip. With today's high speed travel, pulling heavy trailers loaded with boats or campers, you should make a "walk-around" inspection much the same as a small plane pilot does before each trip. Recent studies by several insurance companies have shown that fastening a trailer behind your car more than doubles your chances for a serious accident, and many of these accidents are due to faulty equipment. So pay careful attention to the condition of any trailer you pull. In fact you should have a regular schedule of where-to-look, feel, etc., as you walk around the trailer. Your trailer should be maintenance checked at least before and after each boating or camping season, and following the same schedule in checking and maintaining will simplify your duties.

BEARINGS

Probably the most common problem with trailers is that of wheel bearings burning out or overheating. Each time you stop at a service station, take a moment to run your hand over the wheel bearings. If they're too hot to touch, you've got trouble, so you might as well have them checked. Boat trailers are particularly susceptible to this trouble because of the very nature of their job. You normally pull the loaded trailer for some distance and the metal gets warm and expands. You immediately back the trailer down into cool water, usually over the wheels, and instantly you've got water in the bearings. It's a good idea, if you've got the time, to allow the bearings to cool down a bit before launching the boat. When the boat is launched, pull your trailer out as soon as possible. Any time you allow the hubs in water you stand the chance of causing a leak. Before each season, you should check and repack the wheel bearings with grease. And it's not a bad idea, if you put very many miles on your outfit, to make a middle-of-the season job of it as well.

Repacking a bearing. This is not a difficult job and can be done in minutes. Using a large pair of slip-joint pliers, or a screwdriver used as a wedge, remove the protective dust cover. With the pliers remove the cotter key. Turn the nut off; it should turn by hand or very light wrench pressure, then remove the bearings and clean the inside of the hub, the shaft and bearings with clean, dry cloths. There will probably be quite a bit of rusty water mixed in with the grease. Remove all grease completely, then repack the bearings with new wheel-bearing grease. For a really good job, place the bearing and a handful of grease in a plastic sack and knead the entire mass until you work the grease into the bearing. Apply grease behind the bearings. Examine the bearings, and if they are the least bit chewed, replace them. Put the bearings back in place, pushing them back into the grease. Do not apply too much grease or you run the risk of causing damage to the bearing from the friction of too much grease. You want just enough to keep the bearings covered with a thin film of grease. Usually this means the hub will be about half full when the bearings are in place. Turn the nut back to the same pressure as you took it off. It should be a good hand tight or really light-wrench tight. Make sure you have it turned all the way up and there is no play in the wheel. Line it up with the hole in the shaft and replace the cotter pin. Tap the dust cover back in place, and you're ready to roll. There are now on the market seals that can be attached to the outside of the existing hub which will keep it dry.

HOW TO SERVICE TRAILER BEARINGS

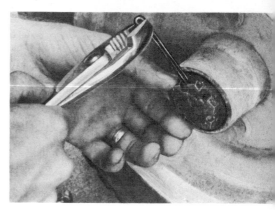

1. Remove dust cover using slip-joint pliers or a screwdriver.

2. Pull cotter key from spindle.

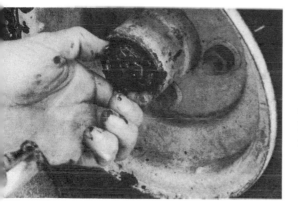

3. Remove nut from spindle and remove bearings. Repack bearings by placing in a plastic bag with lubricant, and kneading. Replace bearings into position.

4. You may have to add a bit of grease to fill bearing cup to half full. It should not be more than half full, however, or you run the risk of burning out the bearing from too much grease.

5. Fit the bearing snugly into position and turn the locking nut hand-tight. Line up the nut with the shaft, and attach the cotter key.

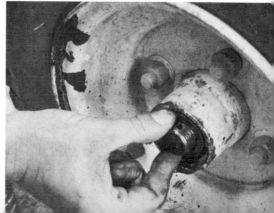

Frequently check the condition of your trailer lights. Replace any burned-out bulbs and rewire any loose connections. Use a tight splice on wires and cover with plastic electrician's tape.

THE LIGHTING SYSTEM

The lighting system on a boat trailer also takes a great deal of abuse from submerging in water, and a burned-out tail or stop light is almost a constant nuisance to many boat owners. There is a solution. You can mount the lights on a bar that fits over the back end of your boat and is held in place by a couple of clamp or spring-type tie-downs. The bar is connected to the trailer with a plug connection, and when you launch your boat remove the bar. Without this type of lighting system, you'll just have to keep replacing bulbs and corroded wires. By all means replace them and have all safety-lighting equipment working properly every time you hook up your trailer.

If your lights are not working, the first spot to check is the connection with your automobile. If this is properly fitted together, the second spot to check would be the bulb. Remove the reflector, take out the bulb and examine it to see if the filament is burned or broken through. Also examine the end of the bulb. If it is heavily corroded, chances are that's your problem. Clean it off with a bit of steel wool or a pencil-type typewriter eraser. If the problem is not in the bulb, trace each wire to its joint and check to make sure all connections are tightly spliced together. It's not a bad idea to put a drop of solder on each. Re-cover each connection with plastic electrician's tape, then tape the wires to the trailer to keep them from flopping and pulling apart.

THE TIRES

Examine the tires carefully—it's not a bad idea to purchase a tire gauge to have on hand to check your tires before pulling out on the road. A flat on a loaded trailer can be a real nuisance. Remember that in most cases your auto jack won't work on the trailer, so you will need to carry a scissor jack. Check your trailer owner's manual for the exact amount of air pressure your tires should carry. You will find they hold two to three times that of your automobile. This you should watch carefully when having service-station attendants check your tires. Don't forget the spare, it can go down in its rack, leaving you with real troubles in case of a flat.

Normally, tire-tread wear on trailers is nominal because there is less friction. But the sidewalls take an awful lot of abuse from flexing, and are the wear areas on trailer tires. Watch the sidewalls carefully for cross checking or deterioration.

THE COUPLER

The coupler on your trailer must withstand tremendously heavy loads, twisting and pulling from trailer swaying, and up and down jolts from rough roads. So if a coupler shows any signs of weakness replace it immediately. The coupler on better trailers will be adjustable from the bottom, to allow you to fit it more closely to the ball. Examine and adjust as needed. Occasionally oil the coupler with 30-weight oil. Examine the ball hitch on your automobile, and make sure it is securely fastened in place. If it becomes covered with grease and rust, go over it with fine steel wool or emery cloth.

Safety chains and coupler should also get an occasional check, retightening or readjusting as needed.

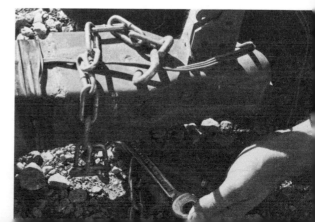

The coupler is the weak link of your trailer, so watch it carefully and replace or repair it immediately if there are any signs of trouble.

Clean the ball hitch on your car with fine No. 400 emery paper to remove the oil, rust and grease.

THE SPRINGS AND TILT-MECHANISM

Examine the springs closely for any signs of abnormal wear. Clean off all the caked-on mud and dirt and lubricate the spring brackets with lightweight oil. If your boat has a tilt-mechanism, check it and lubricate the pivot pins with oil. Also check for wear on the holding pin and spring.

THE WINCH

Lubricate the winch with 30-weight oil. Check the holding bolts, retightening as needed. Examine the winch cable and replace if it shows any signs of wear and tear. This is especially important if the cable is steel, as a worn steel cable can be a definite safety hazard. It can slide through your hands, the tiny slivers cutting your hands like hamburger, or it can flop around and slice a face or leg. Many people use "ski-tow" rope as a winch rope for lightweight boats, and this needs to be replaced at least every three or four years.

Check the springs and clean off any caked-on mud from between them. Lubricate the spring suspension points with a lightweight oil.

If the trailer is a tilt-bed type, check the tilt pins, pivot pins and release spring and lubricate as needed with light oil.

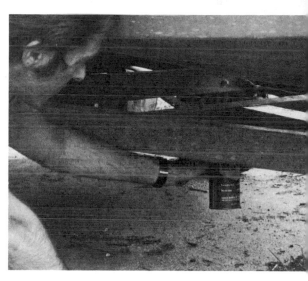

The winch should be lubricated with 30-weight oil and the holding bolts checked frequently for tightness.

123

THE FRAME

Go over the entire frame with a wrench and tighten any loose bolts. If there are any weak welded spots, have them rewelded, then repainted.

If your trailer is used in salt water, hose it down after each trip. Again because of its job of going in and out of water, a trailer rusts fairly fast, and will last quite a bit longer if you can keep it painted, and the worst rust spots removed. Use a stiff wire brush to remove rust spots, then follow with a spray can of rust-inhibiting paint.

Any rusted spots on the trailer frame should be wire-brushed, then rubbed with steel wool and repainted using a rust-inhibiting paint.

Watch the rollers and replace any that are not turning properly or are broken, chipped or cracked.

THE ROLLERS

Replace any rollers that do not turn freely or have become frozen in place. You should also replace any that have cuts or flat spots in them. Examine the padding on the support cradles and replace with scraps cut from carpet remnants. Make sure you get all the old staples out before putting down the new carpet strips.

Metal-spring tie-downs provide the most secure manner of fastening the boat transom to the trailer, but some of them will scar a boat. Encase the metal chain in a section of old garden hose to protect the boat transom.

THE TIE-DOWNS

Use only the proper tie-downs for your boat; otherwise you will have a boat that moves around on the trailer, and a loose bouncing boat is hard on both boat and trailer. A spring activated lever tie-down is usually suggested for the transom. If it must reach any distance under the boat, slide the ends through old sections of garden hose before connecting to the trailer. This protects your boat from the clamp chains. Use shock cord only if you must tie down the front of the boat, rather than a solid no-give tie-down.

Rusted and frozen bolts and fittings can usually be loosened by first spraying lightly with a penetrating oil.

CAMPER TRAILERS

A camper trailer should receive the same kind of walk-around attention and maintenance check as a boat trailer. In addition, it should be prepared in much the same manner as a boat for off-season storage. If possible, store out of the weather, such as in a garage, barn, etc. If you plan to park it in your driveway, check with the local authorities. In some metropolitan areas, it's illegal to park a camper trailer in a driveway for any length of time. If you do park the trailer outside, cover it with a good plastic tarp to keep bird droppings and weather off. Make sure the tarp is lashed down properly so it won't whip in the wind and damage or break a window.

Remove all foodstuff or items that may become damaged or act as a lure for rodents and pests. Also remove all valuables, radios, etc., to prevent theft and vandalism.

It's a good idea to set the trailer up on blocks to take the weight off the wheels. However, an alternative is to occasionally move the trailer a bit to even the weight on the tire treads and prevent a weak area.

Remove or carefully pack and store trailer appliances such as unattached stoves, lanterns, iceboxes, etc. Drain the fuel from any fuel tanks. If the trailer is equipped with bottle gas, make sure the tanks are fully shut off, and there are no leaks at any gas connections. Check this with a brush and a pan of soapy water. A leak will show up as bubbles through the soapy water.

If the trailer is a tent camper, clean off any dirt and grime, using soapy water. Allow to dry thoroughly before packing for storage. Check occasionally during storage to make sure mice haven't gotten in and made a winter nest.

Hose off any road dirt from the trailer's exterior and polish it with a good automobile polish. Touch up any chipped or flaked off paint. Polish all chrome, using a good automobile chrome polish.

Cut any rust from the hitch, using a wire brush, followed by steel wool, then repaint the tongue, using a rust-inhibiting paint. Check the wiring for the tail lights and turn lights, and

A camper trailer-body is held together with many hex-headed screws. Get a good hex-nut driver and keep it on hand for the continuous retightening that is necessary on a well-used camper.

Scratches and nicks can easily be repaired in fiberglass camper bodies using a new gel-coat repair kit. First step is to sand the area well with sandpaper provided.

Second step is to mix solution and spray in place. Sand lightly and you've got a beautiful repair job.

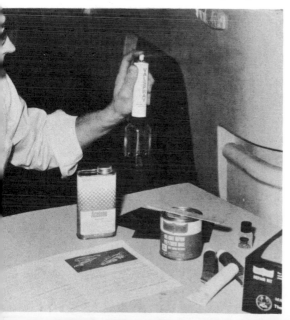

127

All camper upholstery should be cleaned with upholstery cleaner before storing for the winter.

Door hinges and catches should be lightly dusted with a good silicone lubricant before winter storage.

rewire any that are loose or shorting. Check for any bare spots in wiring and cover with plastic tape. Drain water from lines in camper and remove any that may be stored in containers. Clean the upholstery with a good upholstery cleaner, then prop up so air can circulate. Wax all cabinets with a good paste wax, then prop them open.

Zippers of tent campers should be given a light spray of silicone.

To check gas connections for leaks, brush liberally with soapy water. Gas leaks will show up as a series of bubbles.

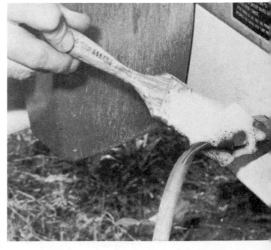

Check your camper for the condition of the gas-line supports. For safety, the gas line should be firmly supported to keep it from bending and popping during travel.

Checking the gas systems. Fortunately, fires in recreational vehicles are few and far between, and that's a lucky thing. When they do happen, the effect is often devastating because of the confined quarters. Small crank-open windows and a lack of multiple escape routes exist in most units. Because of this alone, your vehicle should be kept safe from explosion and fire. Naturally, the greatest danger exists from cooking and heating gas escaping from lines, valves, connections, seams, storage tanks and even appliances. Therefore, gas systems must be inspected periodically, including immediately after purchase. Fortunately, leaking LP gas can easily be detected. It has a distinct, easily identifiable odor. As the gas is heavier than air, it settles, so sniff about in low places if you suspect a leak. A quick way of checking for leaks in connections, fittings and seams is to brush soap suds liberally onto them. Bubbles indicate a leak. If a pilot light goes out, open the vehicle door and allow it to air out before attempting to relight.

8 Gun Care

There have been quite literally thousands of books and magazine articles written about guns. Many of these have actually been about ways of changing a gun to suit a particular taste, rather than just plain how to take care of them, and fix'-'em up when they break down. Unfortunately, plain and simple gun-care rules have been treated so mysteriously that many sportsmen avoid caring for their guns to the point of actually abusing them. As a result, gunsmiths are swamped each year with minor problems that would take the gun owner but a few minutes to repair. On the other side of the coin is the "gun nut" who invariably feels his guns would be improved upon by this treatment or that. However, there are a few basic rules, tips and techniques that anyone can apply to keep his gun in top condition, and without a shop full of expensive tools.

Logically there are two things to protect your gun from: moisture, which causes rust to the metal parts and rotting of the wood; and abrasion, or the wear and tear caused by the parts moving against each other. Theoretically the best way to do this would be to lock your gun up in a controlled-climate gun case and never use it. Naturally this is not possible for most of us. We use our guns as working tools for hobby, for recreation, to provide protection or meat on the table. So the next best thing is to keep them as free from rust and abrasion as we possibly can, and still use them.

STORING GUNS

How your gun is treated while it is not in use has a lot to do with its condition as well as its accuracy. Don't store your guns standing in a clothes closet or down in a damp basement.

They'll only get knocked around or collect moisture. The best spot for storing a gun is a good "locked" rack or case, in a room with plenty of air circulation. One mistake many sportsmen make when storing their guns during the off season is to plug the barrel. Supposedly this keeps out dirt and dust. That it does, but it also keeps air from circulating. This allows moisture to collect, and condensation forms on the inside of

At least once each year, disassemble your gun as completely as possible and thoroughly clean, inspect and lubricate it.

the barrel, causing rusting and pitting. After cleaning your gun, store it muzzle down for some time to allow the excess oil and lubrication to run out. Otherwise, excess oil runs down into the action and eventually soaks into the wooden stock. A gun also should not be stored in a closed leather sheep-wool or flannel-lined gun case. This only traps moisture and again causes rust. If you must store the gun in a leather case, unzip the case partially. Do not put damp guns into such a case even for short periods of time such as for traveling. Always wipe down the gun thoroughly with a lightly oiled cloth. If you remove a gun from its rack or storage to examine it or show it off, always wipe it thoroughly with a lightly oiled cloth or silicone gun cloth before placing it back on the rack. The salty perspiration from fingerprints can cause rust spots overnight. A professional musician of brass instruments can tell you that body moisture can really wreck a metal finish. If you're storing the gun for some period of time, make sure it has a protective coating of rust-proofing oil.

Condensation is the villain in many badly rusted guns, and this can form almost instantly. A hunter's gun is usually used in colder temperatures, sometimes during rain or snow storms. The gun is then brought in out of this cold temperature to the warmer temperature of a cabin or tent and immediately condensation begins to form, not only on the outside, but on the inside of the barrel and the action, in areas where you can't see it. As a result, rust spots can start within hours. A good example of how fast condensation forms is the fogging of your scope or camera lens from your warm breath on a cold day. The solution is simple, don't take your gun out of the cold temperature. If your automobile is nearby, leave the gun locked in it overnight rather than bring it into the cabin. If you're in the "brush," hang your gun just outside the cabin or tent door, out of reach of salt-loving varmints. However, if you prefer to bring your gun inside, wrap it in your coat, and place it just inside the doorway muzzle down for an hour or so to allow it to warm up slowly. A gun should also never be left overnight in a saddle scabbard. The sweat from the horse can penetrate the leather, and a rifle left overnight not only picks up the salty moisture but doesn't allow the scabbard to dry out thoroughly for use the next day.

CLEANING GUNS

To work properly, a gun should be disassembled and cleaned inside and out at least once each season. This not only enables you to keep your gun in proper working condition but allows you to learn how to work on it, a valuable talent to have when a problem develops out in the field.

Preseasonal cleaning.   You will have to be the judge as to how far you should proceed in disassembling your gun. On guns such as double-barrel shotguns, you're limited to removing the barrels from the stocked action. Most pump shotguns, as well as rifles and some pistols can pretty well be disassembled and reassembled without professional experience or tools. When working on a gun there's one gunsmithing rule you should never forget: "Always use the proper screwdriver." Nothing causes more damage than a screwdriver that doesn't fit the screw slot and slips out, chewing up the screw head or the finish surrounding the screw. So have a good supply of assorted screwdrivers on hand.

With the gun disassembled as far as you can take it, spray all parts with a good coating of moisture-displacing, rust-penetrating oil, such as WD-40, and leave it overnight. The next day, spray the parts again and wipe off the loosened oil, rust and grease. You may need to use an old toothbrush to scrub loose some of the more stubborn spots. Wipe and clean all parts dry. Inspect each part for excessive wearing and replace any that may be causing trouble, or that you suspect may cause trouble in the future. Lightly oil all parts with a gun oil.

The first rule of gunsmithing is always to use the proper screwdriver, one that will fit the screw slot without slipping out and gouging the metal or wood.

A serious but common mistake made by many gun owners is to overuse oil and grease. Inletted portion of this old stock is completely soaked and "spongy" from too much oil.

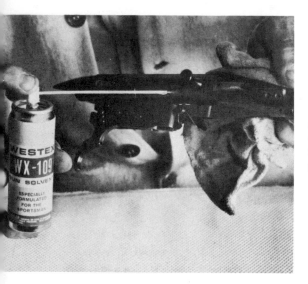

An easy way to apply a light coat of good lubricant in the right places is with nozzle-spray lubricant.

It is very important to use only a slight bit of oil on each part, then place it on a newspaper and allow any excess to drain off. One of the worst and yet most common bugaboos sportsmen commit on their guns is oiling and greasing them too much. In restocking older guns sometimes I've seen cases where the wood next to the action would be so soaked with oil that the wood had become soft and spongy. It seems that many gun owners feel that squirting every available hole and cranny full of oil constitutes "gun care." Once again we go back to one of the basic rules of gun protection; freedom from abrasion. The best way you can achieve this is to have perfectly mating parts without anything between them, and this includes excess oil and heavy grease.

Occasionally check the drawbolt on a pump, automatic or in some cases the newer double shotguns. This is a screw-headed bolt driven from the end of the stock into the gun frame to hold the stock in place. Remove the screws holding the butt plate or recoil pad in place. (This is one of the reasons I never glue a recoil pad on.) Using a long shank screwdriver, check the bolt, tightening if necessary. Be careful not to mar or chew up the screw slot.

With all parts lightly oiled, reassemble the gun, wipe down the exterior with a lightly oiled cloth and place the gun, muzzle down, in a safe place for a day or two to allow any excess oil to drain out of the chamber, action and barrel.

Gun cleaning during season.   Next to this "spring cleaning" in importance is the cleaning and care you give your gun after each hunting trip, or at the end of the day. It doesn't matter whether the gun is a revolver, rifle, shotgun, an automatic, pump, etc., the method of cleaning is essentially the same. The first step is to place a few drops of nitro powder cleaning solvent on a patch, place it on a cleaning rod and draw it through the barrel a couple of times. Follow this with a brass bristle brush of the correct size to fit the barrel. Make at least four or five passes with the brass brush, to loosen the powder residue and lead fouling, then follow with a clean patch dampened with solvent. It's best to clean the barrel from the breech; however, on some guns this, of course, is impossible. If you're still bringing out quite a bit of powder residue on the patch, change it. You may have to change the patch several times to completely clean the barrel. Inspect the barrel and if it is clean and mirror shiny, place a couple of drops of gun oil onto a clean patch and swab the barrel at least a half-dozen times. If you're cleaning a double- or single-barrel shotgun, about the only thing left to do is wipe down the outside with

HOW TO CLEAN A GUN

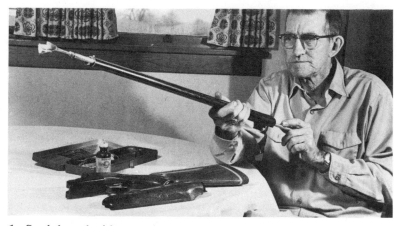

1. Swab barrel with a patch moistened with nitro powder solvent.

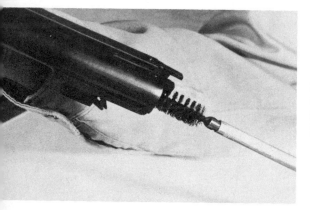

2. Run a brass bristle brush, of the proper size, back and forth several times to cut loose the powder residue.

3. Follow brush cleaning with patches moistened with solvent, swabbing the barrel until the patches emerge clean.

4. Examination should show a mirror-shiny, spotlessly clean barrel. Watch for residues of lead just ahead of the chamber, which the cleaning may not have completely removed.

5. Last step is to reassemble gun and completely wipe outside with a soft cloth slightly moistened with gun oil. Gun should then be placed muzzle down for a while to allow oil to drain out.

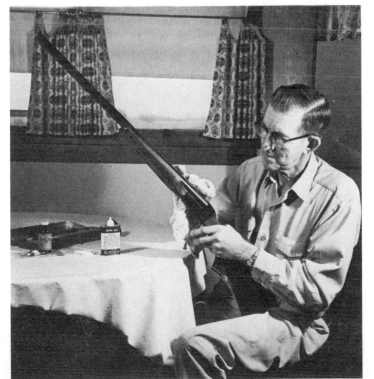

Protecting guns during transport and storage is extremely important. Behind-the-seat gun bag allows guns to be kept free of dust, safe from banging around, and out of sight.

a cloth. However, on revolvers, rifles and automatic and pump shotguns, you'll need to inspect the chamber and action and clean out any grease or debris using a small bristle brush on a wire handle. Dipping the brush in solvent will help cut some of the stuck-on dirt and oil. On self-loading guns, make sure there is no grease or debris in the magazine to later cause trouble with the feeding.

In many cases the only problem with a gun is a screw loosened by vibration, so check all screws and tighten any that have become loose. Replace any that are missing.

If you plan to do any shooting in subzero weather, it's a good idea to disassemble the gun, wash down the parts in lacquer thinner, reassemble and lubricate with dry-spray lubricant or powdered graphite.

With proper care, you'll have very little repair work to do on your gun. There will naturally be an occasional problem, but with a little time and patience most gun problems can be solved by the gun owner, even if he feels he is all thumbs and not a "tinkerer." Although there are many gun problems best left up to a professional gunsmith, there are several jobs you can do in a home shop and without a shop full of high-cost tools. These are the more common problems and how to cope with them. In some cases, it means merely refiling a bit of metal here, or readjusting. In many cases it means you'll need to replace a part with a new one.

One lesson that all amateur gun tinkerers seem to learn on the first try is to proceed very slowly. Do not immediately loosen all the screws in sight, or you may have nothing but a pile of junk, with several springs lost in the far corners of the room. To assure that you'll be able to easily reassemble the gun, lay each piece in order on a sheet of paper as it comes apart and write down the consecutive number by it on the paper.

REVOLVERS

Misfires may be caused by one of several things. For one, the revolver may be out of timing; in other words, the pawl doesn't allow the cylinder to line up with the firing pin and barrel. This can usually be repaired by extending the pawl or lever until it moves the cylinder properly, replacing the old pawl with a new one. Or a broken firing pin may be the cause. If the pin is a part of the hammer, it's a good idea to replace the entire hammer. If the pin is pressed into a bushing and held in place by a pin, it's an easy matter to remove and replace the pin. A misfire may also be caused by a weak or faulty mainspring. Replace with a new one.

If a cylinder does not lock in place, the pawl is probably failing to catch the ratchet. Replace the pawl with a new one or make one to fit from a tiny piece of flat "spring metal."

AUTOMATIC PISTOLS

One of the main problems that develops with auto-feeding pistols is that the metal magazine becomes deformed. That is, the lips become bent, allowing the cartridges to shift out of position, then jam. Replace with a new magazine. If a magazine will not lock in place, check the catch spring. It may need to be replaced. Use solvent and a natural-bristle toothbrush to keep the breech, the face of the slide and the extractor hook of a .22 pistol free of bullet grease and lead scrapings.

RIFLES

Dry firing is a cause of many problems with .22 rimfire rifles. It may cause the firing pin to dent the edge of the chamber, which then causes misfires, or the pin itself may even shatter. The only cure is to have a new barrel put in or have the chamber "sleeved" by a good gunsmith.

Another problem with .22 rifles is that of firing .22 short ammunition in a .22 long-rifle chamber. In time the gases will burn a slight ring in the chamber at the mouth of the .22 short case. When a .22 long is then fired in such a chamber, it expands into the scored ring and causes difficult extraction.

Rough bolt actions may sometimes be cured by smoothing the camming surface. An easy way of doing this is to coat the cam with finest-grit auto-valve grinding compound, place the bolt in the action, hold the trigger back and work the bolt. Remove the bolt and wash it and the rifle thoroughly with a good petroleum solvent.

To keep an autoloading rifle operating properly, the parts must be perfectly clean and lubricated, particularly the chamber. Otherwise, you may cause jamming, feeding and extraction problems.

Pump rifles may not feed because of a slight dent in the

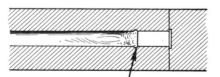

Escaping gas eventually burns ring just ahead of case

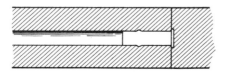

Firing .22 Short ammunition in rifle designed for .22 Long often burns a small ring, caused by escaping gases, just ahead of the case *(above)*. When a .22 Long is used, the case expands into this ring and causes extraction problems *(below)*.

magazine tube. Pound out with a rawhide hammer and a wooden dowel, or replace with a new tube.

If a breech bolt on a pump rifle will not lock in place when the rifle is ready to fire, it may be caused by dirt and grease between the locking lug on the bolt and the recess in the receiver.

SHOTGUNS

On some older and less expensive doubles, the forearm is held in place by a bent, flat spring. This eventually becomes weakened or worn and jumps off or rattles. Lightly hammer the spring to make a tighter fit, or replace if a part is available.

Another problem with older guns is a loose or rattling barrel or barrels. This is usually caused by a worn or bent locking pin, a worn or bent hinge pin, or a barrel lug which doesn't quite engage the hinge pin. If possible, replace with new part

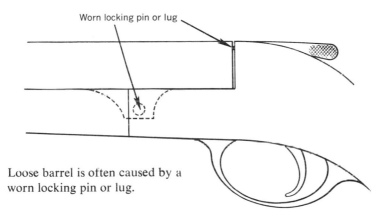

Worn locking pin or lug

Loose barrel is often caused by a worn locking pin or lug.

or one salvaged from a similar gun. If not, you will have to build up one of the surfaces then file down to fit.

Dented shotgun barrels are a common problem with any hunter, and if you have the proper tools, are usually easy to fix. However, any dents in the thick portion of the barrel, next to the breech should be left to professional gunsmiths, as well as those near the muzzle. You will need a dent removing tool for the gauge gun you're repairing.

On shotguns that will not cock, remove the side or bottom cover plates and observe the hammer and sear as the barrels are pushed down. Replace any parts that are worn or missing.

Feeding problems on auto and pump shotguns may also be attributed to bad tubes. Again, remove the dents or replace tubes with new ones.

In colder climates almost any autoloading shotgun can cause trouble. Usually the problem can be traced to poor quality lubrication that may "freeze" parts in place. The only solution is to strip the gun down completely, clean with a good petroleum solvent, then lubricate with a penetrating oil that will not thicken in colder climates.

A dirty or rusty magazine tube can also cause trouble. Polish with very fine steel wool and polishing compounds, then oil lightly.

BARREL OBSTRUCTIONS

Should a patch become caught in your gun barrel, remove it by using a piece of drill rod to which a sheet metal (self-tapping) screw has been soldered. It's not a bad idea to flood the bore with light gun oil. Plug the barrel and leave overnight before attempting to remove the patch. The oil should be poured in from both ends and corks fitted in place.

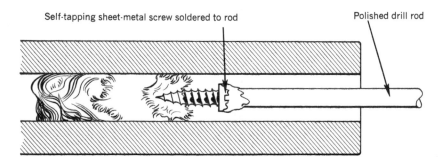

Self-tapping sheet-metal screw soldered to rod   Polished drill rod

Remove stuck cleaning patches with handmade tool.

When using this homemade extractor, don't attempt to remove the entire patch or obstruction at once. Turn it in a bit and tear loose tiny bits of cloth. One thing you can't do is pound out such a problem with a dowel. You'll only force it tighter in place. After you've removed the obstruction, clean the bore with a brass bristle brush, followed by a good gun oil.

Two things best left to the experts are ruptured cases and unfired ammunition which has stuck in the chamber.

BLUEING

The blued coating on a gun is not for appearance alone, it provides protection from moisture and corrosion, and when the blueing becomes worn off your gun is susceptible to rusting. With today's excellent cold blueing solutions and a bit of patience, a beautiful blued finish can easily be applied to your favorite gun. There are hot blues available that can be used by the do-it-yourself gun owner, but they require complete disassembly of the gun and require a bit more finesse in applying. In any type of blueing, hot or cold, the difference in metals from gun to gun and even different metals within a gun will make differences in how the blueing "takes." In most cases, you'll have no trouble getting a good blueing job on the barrel. However, the harder metal of the frame may take a bit more work. Your best bet is to purchase one of the blueing kits that includes not only the blueing but a degreaser solution for cleaning the gun before blueing it.

Cleaning the surface.   The first step for a top reblueing job is to flush the metal surface with the cleaner-degreaser. Follow this with a very fine grit No. 600 wet-or-dry emery cloth or silicone carbide sandpaper and remove all the rust spots and oil and grease. It is extremely important that the metal surface be as clean as possible, because this one factor determines the success you'll have in reblueing. With the gum and rust loosened, flush it off with cleaner-degreaser and wipe the entire gun dry with a soft cloth. It's a good idea to have a new pair of white cotton gloves on hand and, after the cleaner-degreaser step, handle the metal parts with the gloves only. This keeps off fingerprints which can resist blueing.

HOW TO APPLY BLUEING

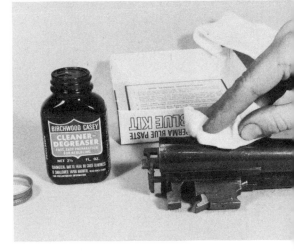

1. Today's cold blueing solutions produce an excellent satin blueing finish with a minimum of trouble. First step is to clean metal surface of oil, grease and dirt with cleaner-degreaser.

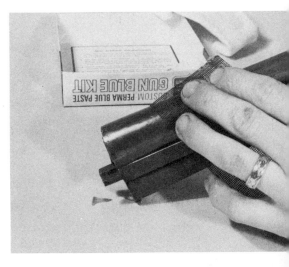

2. Stubborn spots of dirt and grease, as well as patches of old blueing, should be removed using extremely fine steel wool or abrasive paper.

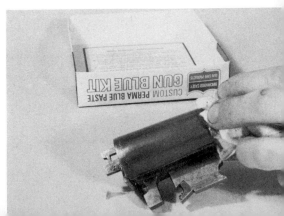

3. Metal is cleaned for the last time with cleaner-degreaser. The metal shouldn't be touched with the bare fingers, or allowed to get dirty before the blueing solution is applied.

4. Blueing solution is swabbed onto the cleaned, prepared metal surface. Blueing works best at warm temperatures, so gun and blueing solution should be slightly warmed befor applying.

5. Surplus blueing solution is removed with a soft cloth, burnished with extremely fine steel wool. It usually takes at least four or five coats of blueing to get a deep, satiny surface.

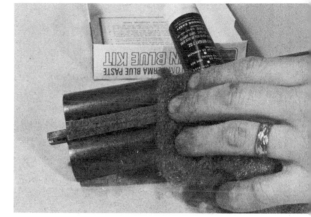

6. Last step is to thoroughly coat the blued surface with a rust preventive. This not only stops blueing solution from further "rusting" the surface, but protects the metal as well.

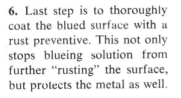

7. Results of a cold blueing job. Only the barrel's front hinge, triggers and guard of this old double have been blued. The frame is case-hardened and does not need a blued finish.

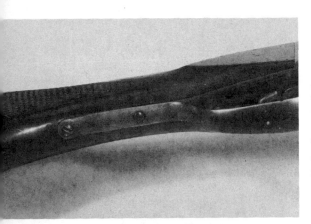

An amazing bit of touch-up work can be done by removing old, chewed-up screws, refiling them to shape, touching them with cold blueing and carefully screwing them back in place.

Applying the blueing. Most cold blueing solutions work best at temperatures above 70 degrees, so it's a good idea to place the metal parts and blueing solution near a warm area such as a furnace heat-register for about thirty minutes. Using the applicator in the kit, or cotton balls pinched in a clothespin, swab the blueing generously over the surface and allow it to "work" for a couple of minutes. Use a soft clean cloth to wipe the surplus blueing off. Follow this with extremely fine steel wool to burnish the blueing to a soft sheen. As it usually takes at least three or four coats, apply additional coats of blueing, wipe off and burnish to get the depth of blueing you need. Cover the entire surface of a piece with each coat of blueing, so you won't have overlaps and blotched areas. One thing not usually furnished in blueing kits, but that will greatly improve the job, is a good rust preventive applied immediately following the last coat of blueing. This not only "sets" the blueing, but protects the metal from further rusting action caused by the blueing solution. The metal parts should be allowed to dry overnight, then a light coat of gun oil is applied to each part and the gun reassembled.

If your gun is an older second-hand gun, check the screws— are they chewed up, the slots in bad shape or are some missing? You can easily remove the screws, refile them to shape, touch them up with cold blue and replace. This one little project can make all the difference in the world in a gun's appearance.

GUN STOCKS

Refinishing a gun stock is usually the first job tackled by the do-it-yourself gun owner. And that's one subject that brings utter confusion. There are probably more recipes for stock finishing than there are guns. I have no doubt that gun stocks have been refinished with everything from peanut butter to old wagon-wheel grease, but basically there are just two finishes. A penetrating finish and a surface finish. Each has good and bad characteristics and each is applied differently.

Applying a penetrating finish. The most popular penetrating finish is linseed oil. This old-time favorite is applied in the same manner today as it was a hundred years ago, and for an "unglamorous" but tough finish it just can't be beat. To apply this finish, place a few drops of boiled linseed oil into the palm of your hand and rub into the stock with enough force and speed to get the stock hot from the friction. The most important rule to remember in applying a linseed-oil finish is to get all the oil worked into the stock, and not leave any remaining on the surface. The rubbed stock should then be placed in a cool, well-ventilated spot and left for a couple of days. When the stock is dry and not "sticky" to touch, repeat the process. It may take as many as a dozen coats to get a good finish on a dense walnut stock, but this finish will really last, and needs only to be rubbed with more oil for touching up. To put a deep sheen on a linseed-oil stock, apply a coat of paste floor wax, then burnish it deeply with clean burlap cloth.

Gun stocks should be stripped of old finish using a good grade of paint or varnish stripper and fine sandpaper or steel wool. Do not use paint scrapers to remove stripper; you run the chance of gouging the wood.

Applying surface finish. The second kind of stock finish is the surface finish and this can be anything from varnish to brush-on lacquer to acrylic or epoxy spray. For this particular type of finish you will first have to seal the pores of the wood. There are two methods of doing this. The first is to rub a solvent-based stain filler into the pores by first applying it thickly with a brush. This is allowed to become slightly dull, then remove with a coarse cloth, wiping first against the grain, then with the grain of the wood. An easier method is to use one of the spray sealers that seals and fills the wood pores. With this type you will need to lightly sand the stock with fine No. 400 silicone-carbide paper after the seal coat to cut off the wood whiskers that have been raised. Most finishes will not stick if an oil-based filler is used.

Of the three most popular surface finishes, varnish is the least protective and the hardest to apply correctly. It is also extremely brittle, as are some other surface finishes. However, the easiest to apply, and if applied correctly, one of the best is a good coating of a spray acrylic finish such as Tru-Oil. To apply this finish, the sanded and filled or sealed stock is suspended from a couple of screws driven into a portion of the stock that will be unfinished. The stock is sprayed holding the can about 6 inches away from the stock and using light dusting coats. Allow the stock to dry overnight then lightly sand with No. 500 fine sandpaper. At least three coats should be applied, sanding lightly between each coat. After the last coat, apply a gun stock wax and buff with a soft cloth. For a stock with a softer sheen, rub the last coat of finish down with a stock rubbing compound. Then apply the stock wax and buff.

If you're stripping a stock for refinishing, the best method is to use a good-quality paint remover and steel wool. Do not use scrapers or coarse sandpaper, or you run the risk of scratching or deeply gouging the wood surface that is softened by the remover.

Many of today's gun-stock polishes and also polishing cloths contain silicones. After these have been applied to a gun stock, it's almost impossible to refinish a stock and get a good finishing job without properly removing the silicone. To do this the stock should be scrubbed with gasoline, benzine or lacquer

HOW TO FINISH A STOCK

1. First step to an easy finishing job is to spray the sanded stock with wood sealer and filler. Apply at least two coats, sanding down to the wood with the first, only lightly with the second.

2. Spray with a good gunstock finish, lightly sand with extremely fine finishing paper, and spray a couple more times. For satiny finish, rub down with compound.

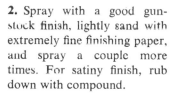

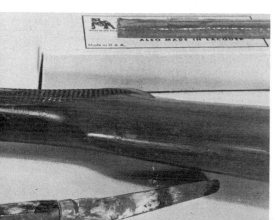

3. Gouges and nicks in stock can be patched with shellac stick. Shellac is picked up with a hot knife blade, dropped into gouge and smoothed to match surrounding finish.

thinner before and after stripping the old finish off. Do this outside. Genuine silicone solvent is safer and better to use.

If a stock has deep dents in it, these can be removed without harming the surrounding finish by ironing them out with a warm electric iron. The iron should be set for synthetics, and a protective sheet of wrapping paper should be placed between the iron and the gun stock. Dampening the dent slightly with a sponge will help on extremely bad cases, or using wet cotton cloth under a very hot iron to force steam into the depressed wood fibers.

Repairing a stock.   Patching a scratched or gouged stock is an easy matter if you have the right equipment. You will need an assortment of shellac sticks, an artist's pallet knife, and a candle or small alcohol lamp. Heat the knife tip in the flame from the lamp or candle. If you use a candle, quickly wipe the soot off the knife blade. Using the tip of the blade, pick up a tiny bit of shellac from a stick of the color that matches your gunstock finish. If the shellac starts to bubble or char, the knife is too hot. Allow the shellac to drop right next to the gouged or scratched areas and quickly pull it into the depression, smoothing it with the knife blade. You'll have to work fast as the shellac sets up mighty quick. With the heated knife quickly smooth the area flush with the surrounding stock. Using a tiny patch of extremely fine wet-or-dry sandpaper and a drop of linseed oil, sand and smooth the patched area to blend in with the stock finish. Apply a polish or wax and buff with extremely fine steel wool.

Replacing a gun stock.   One job that is surprisingly easy to do is replacing a gun stock. This is especially so on pump and automatic shotguns and many rifles. It's a bit harder on double-barrel shotguns because of the amount of inletting needed to fit the stock around the action. Large-caliber rifles are not hard to restock, but the amount of work is greater. The secret in restocking is to buy an unfinished, inletted stock from one of several stockmakers. These are usually called 90 percent or 99 percent inletted; however, they usually require only a little fitting to your action.

Carefully remove the old stock, and place all screws, bolts, etc., in a safe place where they won't be lost. Rough cut the new stock down to match the old one, using wood rasps and machinist's files. In most cases, the stock will come with an oversize grip cap. If you plan to use the cap supplied, flatten and smooth the grip surface with a flat mill file. Place the cap in position and drill a small hole to receive the screw that holds the cap in place. Smear a bit of epoxy glue onto the white spacer as well as the wood and the butt cap, and position the cap and spacer. Place a bit of beeswax on the screw and turn it in place to pull the cap down tightly. Wipe off any glue that may have squeezed out around the edges. After the glue has set, use fine mill files and sandpaper to shape the cap down to fit the wood grip. With the new stock matching approximately the shape of the old one, it's time to inlet it for the action. Mix a bit of cold cream or petroleum jelly with artists' black oil pigment and paint this onto the action. Place the stock into the action or vice versa. Any snug areas or high spots, as may be the case on a rifle barrel channel, will show up as stained spots on the wooden stock. Remove a little wood and try again. For inletting rifle barrels, a barrel inletting rasp is a handy tool. Most inletted stocks will require very little cutting to fit the action and stock together. With the stock and action fitted together, mark any areas where the wood must be cut down to meet the metal properly. Remove the action and cut the wood down just a little at a time.

With the stock fitted to the action and roughly shaped to the size of your old stock, lay the old stock in position over the new one and mark the new stock for length. Make sure you have the old stock positioned exactly over the new one, or the "drop" will be a bit different and it may throw your shooting off. Cut off the stock to the right length using a hand saw or band saw. Be extremely careful to keep the saw at right angles to the stock so the end of the butt doesn't cant to one side or the other. When the saw is almost through the cut, turn the stock over and start a cut from the opposite side to meet the first cut. This will keep you from splintering off a large chunk of the lower edge of the stock as the saw breaks through. You can then use a good flat mill file to smooth and straighten the cut. If you're using the butt plate instead of a recoil pad,

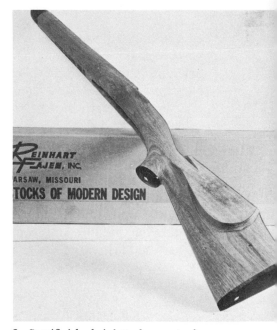

1. First step in fitting new stock is removal of old stock—an easy job on most rifles and pump or automatic shotguns. Large-shank screwdriver is needed to loosen drawbolt on shotgun.

2. Semifinished, inletted gun stocks come in all shapes, sizes to fit almost any make or type of gun, require only minor fitting in most cases. Most of work involves finishing and shaping.

3. New stock is shaped with machinist's files and wood rasps. For a first-time job, stick pretty closely to shape of old stock, particularly if you're hitting with the gun.

4. Position grip cap in place and drill hole to receive cap screw. Coat cap and spacer with epoxy glue and glue and screw cap in place. File and rasp it down to fit wood grip.

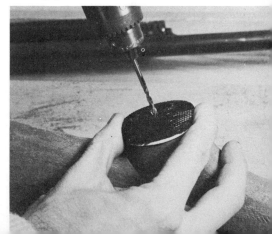

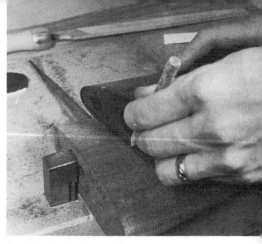

5. Shotgun stock is inletted or fitted into action, or vice versa with a rifle stock. Rifle stock inletting usually takes a bit more work to get the barrel channel properly fitted. Stock is filed down to fit flush with metal surface.

6. Old stock is positioned on new stock and new stock marked for length. Make sure stocks are in perfect alignment so the new stock will have the correct drop.

7. Stock is cut to length using a handsaw or band saw. Make sure you keep the cut square. Otherwise the buttplate or recoil pad will cant to one side.

8. Cut-off end of stock is filed perfectly flat and smooth using a good mill file.

9. Butt plate is temporarily screwed in place, plate and end of stock rasped and filed to make a perfect fit of plate and end of gun stock.

mount it in place with screws only, no glue, and shape the plate and stock together with a wood rasp, then follow with a mill file. Sand the entire stock as smooth as possible and apply the finish.

CHECKERING

You may have an older gun on which the checkering needs refurbishing, or you may have replaced a stock and it needs checkering. But in any case, don't back off from this fun and relaxing job. You may think you could never accomplish such an exacting and detailed job, but actually checkering is about 25 percent skill and 75 percent patience. If you go carefully and take your time, you'll have a creditable checkering job the first time. However, it's a good idea to do a practice a checkering job on an old gun stock rather than your new one.

Although you can hold the stock for checkering in a vise, a checkering cradle makes the job about twice as easy. So if you plan on checkering more than pistol grips or shotgun foreends, make a checkering cradle. You will also need a single cutter and spacing cutter checkering tool, diamond template, small file for sharpening the cutters and small brass bristle brush.

Checkering is one job that's easy and fun, requires about 25 percent skill and 75 percent patience. Homemade checkering cradle makes job much easier.

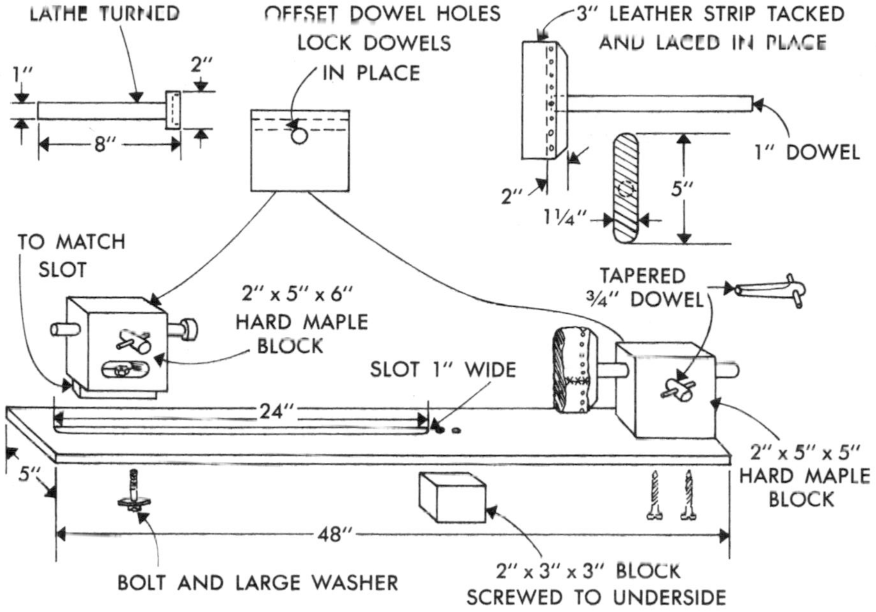
LATHE TURNED
1"
2"
8"
OFFSET DOWEL HOLES
LOCK DOWELS
IN PLACE
3" LEATHER STRIP TACKED
AND LACED IN PLACE
1" DOWEL
2"
1¼"
5"
TO MATCH
SLOT
2" x 5" x 6"
HARD MAPLE
BLOCK
TAPERED
¾" DOWEL
SLOT 1" WIDE
24"
2" x 5" x 5"
HARD MAPLE
BLOCK
5"
48"
BOLT AND LARGE WASHER
2" x 3" x 3" BLOCK
SCREWED TO UNDERSIDE

Plans for building a checkering cradle.

Making a pattern. The first step in checkering is to select a pattern to suit the particular gun. This is made easy by the use of stick-on patterns that are available, or you can make a rubbing of a pattern from an already checkered gunstock and transfer this pattern to your gun. To make a rubbing, place a piece of tracing paper over the checkering and rub the paper briskly with a soft lead pencil. The checkering pattern will come through as a "rubbing." After determining the pattern you wish and transfering it to your gun, mark the first diagonal line using a flexible steel or plastic strip as a guide. Then using the spacing tool, cut the second or following cut. Continue making cuts until you reach the border of the pattern. Turn the stock around and cut to the opposite border, completing all the lines in one direction. Use the brass brush to keep the chips out of the way. Do not worry about cutting the lines deep, just get them marked in place.

HOW TO CHECKER A GUN STOCK

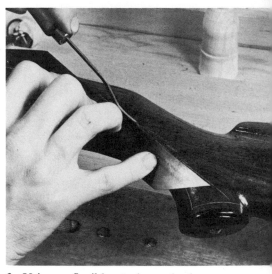

1. Checkering pattern is traced onto gun stock, carefully marked in finish with tip of scriber or pencil.

2. Using a flexible steel or plastic straightedge strip, first diagonal line of checkering diamonds is cut. Single cutter is used to make cut.

3. Spacing cutter is used to make succeeding lines. The cutter works like a farmer's plow. One side of the cutter rides in the previously cut line to guide the new cut.

4. Lines are cut in one direction, then diamond template is used to mark the opposite lines of diamond. Single cutter is used to clean and cut lines deeper.

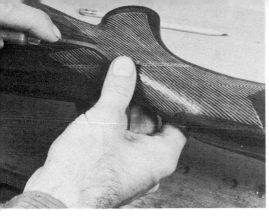

5. Again spacing cutter is used to make successive cuts.

6. Single cutter is used to deepen cuts and sharpen them next to border of pattern.

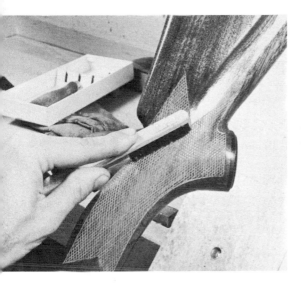

7. Small, stiff bristle brush is used frequently to keep chips out of lines.

9. Checkered area of stock is spray-finished to match rest of the stock. Be careful of overspray in checkering. Runs can be crested quite easily in the tiny grooves.

8. Single cutter and small wood chisel is used to cut a single border line around pattern.

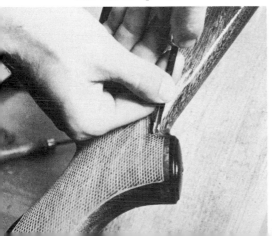

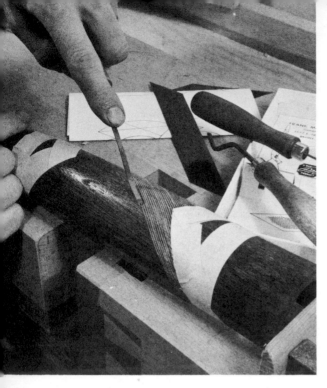

A kit including checkering tools and diamond templates is available from most gun-supply houses.

Using a diamond template designed for checkering, cut the first line in the opposite direction. Again use the spacing tool to cut the following lines, and actually that is all there is to it. When you've cut all the diamonds, go back over them with the single cutter and even up their depths. Then using the single cutter and a tiny chisel, cut a V-border around the pattern to give the checkering a more finished appearance. Using the brush, clean out the lines. Smooth over the checkering with fine sandpaper and apply a finish to match the existing finish.

SLING SWIVELS

Maybe you need sling swivels on your deer rifle. No, this isn't a particularly difficult job, and the only tools you will need are a drill, powered or hand, and a screwdriver. Remove the action from the stock and place the stock upside down in a vise. The vise should be padded to keep from marring the stock. For the rear swivel, drill a hole about 2½ to 3 inches from the toe of the stock. The hole should be just slightly smaller than the swivel screw. Place a bit of beeswax on the screw and turn it into the stock. You may have to use a screw-

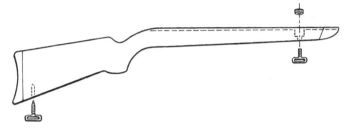

Install sling swivels in buttstock and fore-end.

driver blade in the slot for turning leverage. For the fore-end swivel, you will first have to measure with the sling for the proper position. This is determined by the length of sling, personal preference, etc.; however, usually it is located from 3 to 4 inches back from the end of the fore-end. Two holes will need to be drilled for this swivel. A small hole is drilled completely through the stock up into the barrel channel. Then a larger hole, the size of the nut that fits on the bolt is counterbored down from the inside of the barrel channel just enough to allow the nut to clear the barrel. The nut must not touch the barrel or the rifle will shoot just a bit high. The nut should be pushed into the hole, the bolt threaded up into it to fit snugly and the rifle reassembled.

RECOIL PADS

Installing a recoil pad on a gun is an easy matter. If the stock is too long, or short, you can easily correct this while installing the pad. After determining the correct length of your stock, position the recoil pad (parallel with the butt plate) the length you wish the stock to be and mark with a pencil. Make sure this cut-off line is parallel with the line of the butt plate. Wrap masking tape around the stock with the edge following the cut-off line. Then tape the entire stock except for the cut-off piece. You can use either a hand saw or band saw for cutting off the excess. If you use a band saw, you will have to wedge up the opposite end of the stock to keep the cut square with the centerline. If you use a hand saw, position the stock in a

APPLYING A RECOIL PAD

1. First step in applying recoil pad is to position pad in place, parallel with buttplate, and mark a fine line the length the stock should be cut.

2. Masking tape is wrapped around stock following edge of cut-off mark. Entire stock is then wrapped with tape.

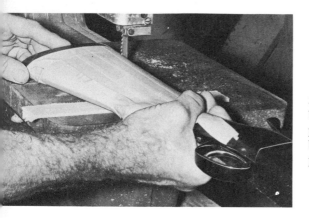

3. Stock is cut to length. If a band saw is used, the front portion of stock will have to be shimmed up to keep cut parallel.

4. Cut-off end of stock is sanded or filed perfectly flat and square.

5. Pad is positioned in place, marked from the underside.

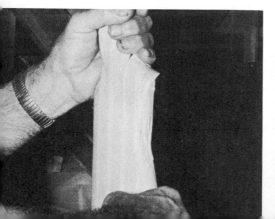

6. Excess pad is ground or filed off.

7. Pad is positioned in place, screw holes marked with sharp awl and drilled with a small bit.

8. Using a fine-blade screwdriver the pad is screwed in place. Beeswax on screws will aid in driving them.

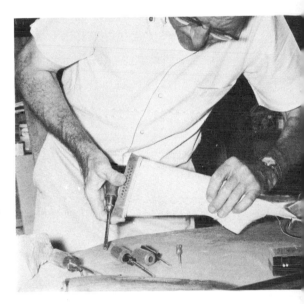

10. Tape is removed from stock and any nicked spots in stock finish are touched up.

9. Pad is ground and shaped with fine files and sander.

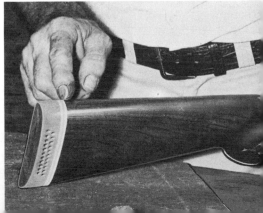

padded vise before cutting. The recoil pad is positioned on the cut-off stock and marked from the underneath side. The excess edge of the pad is ground off with a belt sander or filed off with a machinists' file. The pad is then repositioned, marked for the screw holes and the holes bored. The rough-ground pad is screwed in place. If you wish to glue the pad on, use epoxy glue. The pad is then finished ground or filed down to the exact shape of the stock, being extremely careful of the stock finish. Sanding the recoil pad with a finish sander will remove any file or rough sander marks. Using a finish compatible to that on the stock, touch up any tiny areas that you may have nicked while grinding the pad.

9 Scopes and Cameras

SCOPES

One of the easiest-to-care-for tools a sportsman owns is his rifle scope. In fact, today's modern rifle scopes are so well-designed and precision-made that they require practically no care. On the other hand, although the scope has been one of the greatest helpmates of today's hunter, it is probably one of the least understood tools. All modern quality scopes are sealed against moisture and dust, and their "optics" should not be tampered with or disassembled. If a scope needs to be repaired "internally," send it back to the factory.

About the only care normally required is a careful cleaning when you clean your gun, or in the case of binoculars, after each trip. This takes but a minute or two. Wipe the dirt and dust from the outside and clean the lenses with either a lens cloth provided with the scope or with a cotton swab dipped in either alcohol or acetone. Keep the lenses covered with the lens caps as much as possible for protection from dust as well as sharp objects.

Installing a scope. Whether on a .22 or high-powered rifle, in most instances this is actually not much of a chore, but a fun job. However, it requires that you carefully follow the instructions included with the scope mounts. Many .22's have grooves cut in the top of the receiver, and mounting a scope on these can be a snap, requiring only minutes.

Loosen the clamping screws on the scope mount until the scope will slide easily onto the grooves in the receiver. Position the scope to achieve the correct eye relief. For the best results this must be done by you or the individual that will normally be shooting the rifle. Look through the scope with your cheek in a normal shooting position. Quickly glance away, then back

Binoculars and rifle scopes should be cleaned after each trip, using the cleaning cloth provided, or with a soft cloth and alcohol.

Installing scopes on most modern .22 rifles is easy. The scopes are mounted with a vise-like mount that clamps onto grooves cut into the top of the rifle receiver. Merely tighten in place with a screwdriver.

into the scope. You should be able to pick up the sight picture immediately without moving your head around. If you see a partial picture or the edges are blackened and blurred, slide the scope backward or forward on the grooves to achieve the best sight picture. The eye relief or distance from the rear end of the scope to your eyebrow should normally be around three inches. Although this is not as important on a .22, for safety's sake on a high-powered rifle the scope should be no closer. With a vise, clamps or even books, position the rifle level, using a small carpenters' level on the top of the receiver. About 30 feet away position a white card with a horizontal black line drawn with a ruler and marking pen. Make sure the black line is positioned level. Check the cross wire on the scope and when you're satisfied with the sight picture, tighten the screws on the clamp to fasten the scope in place in the grooves. Use a good screwdriver that properly fits the screws and tighten as tight as possible.

In positioning scope on any rifle, whether .22 or high-power, the eye relief, or the distance from your eyebrow to the back end of the scope, should not be less than 3 inches.

Focusing a scope. Because everyone's eyes are different, scopes are focusable by use of a rotating eyepiece. This is usually held in place by a knurled ring. Loosen the ring, then turn the eyepiece in or out to focus. Focusing need only be done once, when you first install your scope. Although focusing is an easy task, it must be done properly. In focusing your scope, you should use your eyes as you would for distance scanning, not on the scope itself.

You should have an aiming spot several hundred feet or more distant, and also be able to quickly point the scope at the sky or a blank wall. The object is to focus the reticle, not the distant scene or object, with your eyes in the normal state you would use when shooting. First turn the locking ring several turns to move it out of the way. Point the scope at the sky or a light object and turn the eyepiece until the reticle is as clear and sharp as possible. Now look away from the scope at a distant object. With your eyes focused on this object look

165

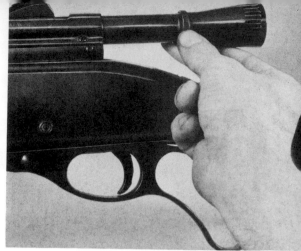

Rifle scopes must be focused by the user. The first step is to loosen the knurled locking-ring on the back end of the scope. Then move the focusing piece by turning to the right or left.

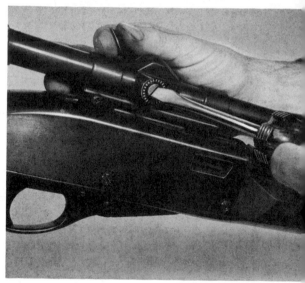

Windage and elevation adjustments are standard on practically all scopes, can be turned with a large screwdriver or coin after removing the protective caps.

To move a .22 rifle scope backwards or forwards after clamping it to the rifle receiver, loosen the scope rings holding screws and slide scope in direction desired.

through the scope at the reticle. If the reticle appears a bit blurred, turn the eyepiece just a slight bit, usually clockwise, then try the distant object again, then back to the reticle. Keep doing this until you have the scope adjusted so that the reticle is immediately sharp when you glance into the scope. This is the only way you can fully utilize the quick-sighting abilities of your scope and be able to pick up distant running game quickly and easily. If your scope is a target or varmint model with parallax adjustment, it should be focused in the same manner. Use the parallax adjustment only to focus the target in sharply. The parallax adjustment will naturally need to be done each time the target distance is changed.

Mounting a scope.   Mounting a scope on a high-powered rifle is somewhat different, and each rifle requires a slightly different technique. However, there is somewhat of a standard procedure that you can follow. On some rifles you can mount the scope directly over open sights, but on others these will have to be removed. This is an easy job of tapping the sights out of their dovetail slots, using a small punch and light hammer. However, be sure to punch them out from the left side, as most dovetail slots are tapered to the left.

Most rifles manufactured today are drilled and tapped for scope sights at the factory with "plug" screws concealing the scope holes. Scope mounts and ring bases are made in standard sizes to fit these screwholes. So about the only problem of scope mounting on many high-powered rifles is tightening the screws properly so the mounting screws will not loosen in the field, causing inaccuracies and missed shots. This is not a particularly hard job, but there are a few tricks to getting the screws properly tightened.

Place the rifle in a good vise, well-padded to protect the rifle. Using a small level, position the rifle as level as possible. Remove the filler screws and make sure they and all mating surfaces of the mounts and rifle receiver are free of oil. A bit of alcohol swabbed on with a piece of cotton will remove most grease and dirt. Screw the ring base or bases in place. A drop of fingernail polish or "Loc-Tite" in the screw holes is the secret for anchoring the screws more firmly. Using a screwdriver that properly fits the screw slots, carefully turn the screws down as tightly as possible. Tapping the handle of the screwdriver lightly with a hammer as you make the final tightening will also help in driving the screws tightly.

Rifles that are not drilled and tapped can be "scoped" by the "tinkerer," but it takes a few more tools and a heck of a lot more time. One tool that is almost a necessity for drilling and tapping a rifle action for a scope is a drill press. It doesn't have to be a complicated machinists' press, even a small stand supporting a variable-speed drill will work. But you must have some means of keeping the drill square with the surface of the metal. Finding the position to mount the scope ring mounts or mount on the top dead-center of a rifle receiver is actually the trickiest part of the job.

If your rifle has a dovetailed slot for the rear mount as the Remington in the photo, you can fasten the rear mount in the center and use a rubber band to hold the front of the scope down, move it back and forth, sideways, or however you need to line the scope up. This should only be done if your scope is new and has not been turned out of alignment. The alternative is to use a cross level and a parallel clamp, working off the flat underside of the receiver. Once you've found the top dead center, mark the position of the mounts. Then using a good center punch, mark for each hole. Be careful, as the case-hardened surface of some receivers can shatter a punch, driving pieces into your hand. If your rifle is one of the earlier Springfields or Remingtons, particularly the O3-A3, you'll have trouble starting a hole in the receiver, because the receiver metal is so hard. These receivers require spot annealing for the holes.

However, the best method for a beginning tinkerer is to carefully grind off a bit of the case-hardened surface in the screw hole, using a small stone in a hand grinder. Then, using the drill called for in the instructions for your mount, carefully drill the holes. Nitro Powder Solvent, which you ordinarily use to clean your gun, is a good lubricant. If you have bad luck and snap off a drill in a hole, take a small punch and rap it

HOW TO MOUNT A SCOPE

1. The first step in mounting a scope on a rifle that does not have factory-installed mounting screws is to remove the action from the stock.

2. Most military and iron sights are dovetail mounted and must be tapped out using a small brass pin and lightweight hammer. Remember to drive from the left.

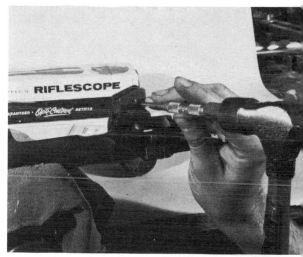

3. To mount a scope properly, you must find the top-dead center of the rifle receiver. There are two ways: using parallel clamps off the bottom of the receiver, or a level if the top of the receiver has a flat spot.

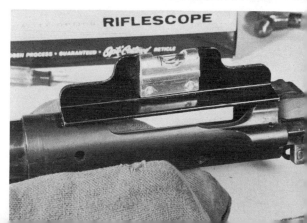

4. Using a good steel punch, center-punch for the mount screws. Be extremely careful to do this one job as accurately as possible.

5. Using a drill chucked in a drill press and turning at the slowest speed possible, carefully drill the center-marked hole to the depth desired. Go slowly and carefully and use a good lubricating agent. Many gunsmiths use Nitro Powder Solvent.

6. The next and most tedious step is to thread the hole with a tap. Chuck the tap into a drill press, but do not use power. Turn it only by hand and very slowly, backing up each time it squeaks and adding more cutting solvent such as Nitro Powder Solvent.

7. With the holes all bored and tapped, clean the mounting surfaces and the holes thoroughly with alcohol or lacquer thinner. All surfaces must be free of dirt, oil and burrs for a good mount.

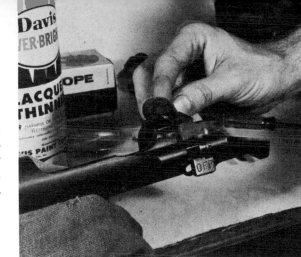

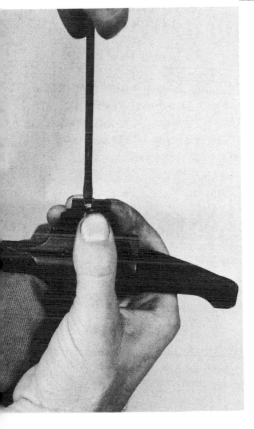

8. Position the mount in place and carefully start the screw. Fasten the mount temporarily.

9. With the mounts temporarily fastened, mount the ring clamps on the scope.

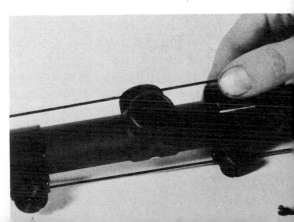

10. Mount the scope on the rifle in the general position you would normally be using it. Clamp the rifle in a vise and boresight it by positioning the barrel so you can see a target center through it about 30 feet away. With the scope's internal adjustments untouched, use light brass or cardboard shims to move the scope to line up fairly close with the target center.

11. When you find the exact position you wish for the scope, mount it permanently in place using a bit of Epoxy or Loc-Tite as a bedding compound on the screws.

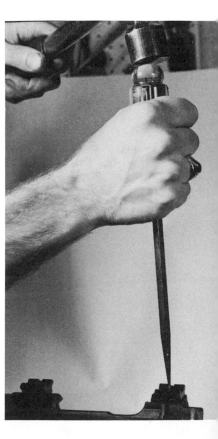

12. To attach a scope properly, it must be fastened securely enough to keep from shifting from the recoil and knocks. One good trick is to lightly tap on the mount screws as you turn them in place.

sharply. Chances are you'll shatter the drill and can then shake it out of the hole. The next step is to tap the hole to accept the mount screw. Use a starting tap in the number called for in the instructions. It's a good idea to clamp your receiver to the drill-press table while you're drilling. Then when the hole is bored, remove the drill from the drill-press chuck and insert the tap. Using hand power only, not the motor, carefully turn the tap into the hole, again using the Nitro Solvent, or ordinary lard or bacon fat, as a lubricant. When the threads have started, switch to a bottoming tap and finish threading the hole. If a tap breaks off in a hole bored with a bottom opening, it's usually no problem. Merely rap the tap with a small punch and it will usually shatter. However, if it is in a bottoming hole, you've got problems. About the only thing you can do is to rap it sharply to break it up. Then, using a tiny drill, try to work the pieces loose.

With the holes drilled, mount the scope temporarily and fasten the rifle into a padded vise. Position the barrel to point at the center of a target about 25 feet away. Check the position of the scope. In many cases you'll need to shim under one corner of one or the other blocks to work the scope halfway into aligning with the target center. For shims use light cardboard coated with shellac or small pieces of brass shim stock. When you're satisfied with the position of the scope, remove it. Place a drop of Loc-Tite on each screw, reposition the shims needed and refasten the scope blocks in place. Use plenty of pressure and the proper size screwdriver to get the blocks as tightly fitted as possible. Some gunsmiths like to "bed" these blocks with a bit of epoxy glue, and it definitely gives you a better fit with the gun if you've got a shim or two in place. Remount the scope and recheck it for position. If you're satisfied, set it aside at least overnight before adjusting further.

Sighting the rifle.   The next step is to sight in the rifle and scope. With a .22 this is a simple matter. Set up a target with a large backstop at 25 yards. If the rifle is a bolt action, it can be sighted in roughly by "boresighting." Remove the bolt and place the rifle in a padded vise. Place an aiming point such as a 1-inch black circle on a piece of paper on the backstop. Move the rifle until this spot is centered in the bore. Then position the center of the reticle on the scope on the aiming point without moving the rifle. This may require tiny shims under the scope on some rifles. On rifles without removable bolts, you'll have to use a small angle mirror such as a dental mirror to initially set up the base sighting. "Shoot" a couple of shots to determine where you are shooting. However, remember to have a pretty large backstop because you won't know exactly where your shots will hit.

The rifle should be shot from a well-padded rest and preferably under calm weather conditions. Turn the windage and elevation knobs, using a large screwdriver or coin in the direc-

Bore sighting a rifle.

With the scope permanently mounted, boresight it again use the internal (elevation and windage) adjustments to r it. Shoot a series of three shots and sight it in.

After a .22 rifle has been initially sighted in, an amusing way of fine-tuning the sighting is to shoot at playing cards stuck with edge towards you at 25 yards.

tion of the arrows to move the point-of-impact to the right or up. If you must move it to the left or down, turn the adjustment in the opposite direction. With your rifle properly sighted in at this distance, you may wish to move it to the distance you will normally be shooting at. This means you would normally do final sighting in at 100 yards.

Move the target this distance and fire a group of three shots. Then readjust the adjustments in order to zero the rifle in. A .22 can also be initially sighted in at distances shorter than 25 yards—a fact somewhat leaned upon by a gunsmith buddy of mine who initially sights in .22 rimfires in his basement, of course with a lead-sand backstop. He then checks for accuracy of the "sighted scope" by splitting playing cards facing him edgewise. An impressive but easily done feat if the rifle is sighted in at those close ranges. The rifle is then taken outside to a 100-yard range and zeroed in. However, if most of your .22 shots are taken at short ranges, you'll do better to sight in your rifle at a final range of 25 yards. Sighting in a high-powered rifle is basically the same; however, the final zeroing in should be done on a range of 200 yards.

CAMERAS

When it comes to repairing your camera, the general rule is don't. Even the seemingly simple can sometimes turn into the impossible without the correct tools and knowledge of just how a fixture is fitted to the camera. This does not, however, mean you should neglect your camera. It should occasionally be cleaned carefully and thoroughly and there are some repair jobs you can tackle. In fact, most camera faults can be traced to dirt, sand, grit or moisture in the mechanism or on the lens. This may slow down the shutter, cause mirror returns and escapement mechanisms to stop working and even stop a flash shoe from functioning. A problem that frequently develops is a small nick or a piece of foreign matter on the film rollers scratching the negative. Once again, a careful cleaning does the trick. One problem that frequently develops on Polaroid cameras is that the rollers gum up and may require cleaning to assure that the film pulls freely out of the film pack for developing.

Cleaning a camera.   Occasionally inspect and clean your camera. This not only helps in keeping the dust and lint down for better photographs, but enables you to spot loose or missing screws or small problems before they become big ones. In fact this cleanup inspection is essential for the professional photographer and is done before each assignment by most commercial photographers. A small rubber ball blower with brush attached is one of the best items for cleaning the lint and dust from inside your camera.

Do not tear down the camera to clean it. Merely open the back and clean what you can reach easily. Another good item is a camel's-hair brush that is kept in an old toothbrush tube and used entirely for the cleaning job alone. This is handy for flicking lint out of the tightest crevasses. Clean the camera lens with lens paper only. If it is badly smeared or has raindrops, fingerprints or oil on it, moisten one of the papers in a bit of lens-cleaner fluid or alcohol and dampen the lens. Lightly wipe the lens dry with a clean, dry paper. Occasionally the inside of the lens may become dirty and smeared and may also need to

To clean your camera, don't tear it down to the point you can't get it back together again. Leave that for the experts. Merely remove what you can without trouble and clean it thoroughly.

be cleaned with the fluid. If the lens is fixed in the camera body, wrap the cleaning tissue around the end of a pencil eraser. Touch it a bit with the cleaning fluid and lightly swab the lens. Again remove the wet tissue, replace it with a clean, dry one and lightly dry the lens. A removable lens is naturally easily cleaned. The outside of the camera body should be cleaned with tissues moistened in the lens-cleaning fluid, then again dried with fresh, dry tissues. Inspect the camera thoroughly and retighten any loose screws with a tiny screwdriver, not a pocket-knife blade.

A set of watchmaker's screwdrivers and a tiny pair of tweezers make work on the tiny screws of cameras much easier. Many times the tiny screws work loose and merely need tightening.

A camel's-hair brush, kept for that purpose only, is excellent for flicking dust and lint out of the camera interior. It can be kept in toothbrush tube.

To clean a camera lens that has become extremely dirty, use a good lens cleaner and lens-cleaning paper. Work slowly and carefully.

Really bad spots on the interior of a camera and a mirror that's hard to reach can be cleaned with a piece of lens paper wrapped around a pencil eraser and held with a rubber band, then dipped in lens cleaner.

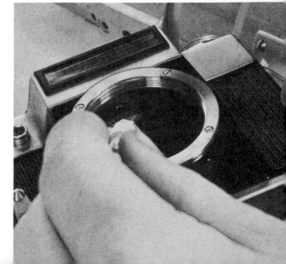

A pinhole in a bellows is easily repaired using cloth mending adhesive. Apply it sparingly or it will crack and eventually pop off.

Any spots where flat black paint has come off inside of camera should be touched up with small brush and india ink. Otherwise they may cause light streaks on your photos

Repairing a camera. A bellows camera should frequently be checked for tiny pin holes that may develop in the folds of the material. This is easily done by holding the opened camera between you and a bright light in an otherwise darkened room. Tiny holes or tears in the bellows can easily be repaired with fabric cement. However, do not apply the cement too thickly or it will crack off. Scratches or any chipped paint on the inside of the camera should be touched up with a tiny brush and some india ink or flat black paint. The spots shouldn't be allowed to stay, as they can cause reflections and resulting light streaks on your photos.

Protecting a camera.   One of the most perplexing problems confronting the camera-toting sportsman is keeping the camera safe from water. This can be as simple as placing it in double-plastic garbage bags, or in an expensive watertight case specially made for photographic equipment. However, one of the most economical and best-working is an Army-surplus ammo case. This can be made even more effective by placing Styrofoam in the bottom and top to cushion the camera and equipment against shocks. Painting the case a bright color such as fluorescent orange or bright yellow helps identify it and makes for a speedy recovery in the advent of swamping or losing it during an especially rough canoe or boat ride. And this brings

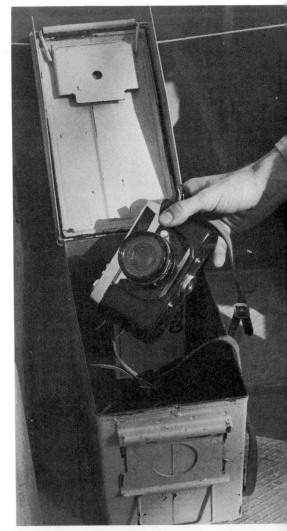

Any outdoorsman carrying a camera in a boat, canoe, or on horseback, should have a stout, waterproof container for his cameras. Case shown is a surplus ammunition case that has been brightly painted.

up the inevitable. The worst that can happen is to lose a camera overboard and not have it in a watertight case. However, if you carry a camera in the field, it may happen, and when it does you've got only one recourse. As soon as possible tear down the camera as far as you possibly can and place the items in a cool, dry spot to allow them to air dry. Constantly keep checking and working the mechanisms to keep them from freezing up as the water dries up, drying the light film of lubricant on the mechanisms. Using tissues taped to the end of a pencil or brush end, reach down into any tight spots and "sponge" up as much water as possible. A packet of silicone drying agent will help greatly in drying out the water, especially if placed inside the camera or down in the center of a long telephoto lens, one of the last-to-dry spots. Then, as soon as you get back home, take your camera into your dealer and give him full details of how the dunking took place. If you're lucky, you may get by without too much trouble, but sometimes a dunked camera can be a traumatic experience.

Miscellaneous. If you have troubles with a flash or electronic flash unit, the first thing you should check is the condition of the batteries. Replace any batteries you suspect are weak. It's a good idea to keep a spare battery on hand, as well as a capacitor. If the battery is good it may be the capacitor causing the trouble. However, capacitors will usually last for a long time. If you have checked both capacitor and batteries, the next probable trouble spot is either the cord connection, or in the case of a hot shoe flash, the connecting shoe. Sometimes cleaning these connections with a solution of vinegar applied with the tip of a small brush will help.

One of the best ways you can protect the lens on your camera is to place a "haze" filter over it and leave the filter on all the time. The filter will not only cut down on some of blueness and smoky appearance of some long-distance landscape shots, but will act as a protector for your lens in case you drop the camera or run into brush. Or, a lens hood will protect your lens and prevent stray light rays from fogging your pictures when you shoot toward the sun.

First spot to check for trouble on flash is battery, then capacitor. Next check connections. Clean battery ends and connections using a pencil-type typewriter eraser.

Condensation can cause the same problems with a camera that it can with a gun, so protect the camera from moisture and condensation problems and you won't have as much trouble with rust and resulting damage. If the camera is to be used outside, leave it outside or allow it to warm up slowly before bringing it into a warm cabin or tent from a cold temperature.

Some cameras may even refuse to operate in extreme cold, the heavier lubricants slowing up the mechanism and maybe even freezing them. In this case don't force the mechanism or you may break tiny springs or parts.

Lenses of shooting glasses get a lot of hard abuse. Most common trouble is a lens popping loose. It can be reglued with household cement.

10 Decoys and Blinds

Waterfowling is indeed a world by itself, and for many hunters making and maintaining "blocks" is half the fun. What better way of spending a long winter evening than dreaming of flight after flight of ducks, wings set, barreling down into your decoy stool, while you repair a battered bluebill body or repaint a hen mallard? Decoys are subjected to the worst of conditions with freezing temperatures, sleet and snow, not to mention being knocked and bounced around in a loaded boat or automobile. All of this naturally takes a toll on your supply of workable blocks, breaking some, chipping and scraping paint off of others. As any successful waterfowl hunter knows with today's high-pressure hunting, you need an "edge," and a freshly cleaned and repaired set of decoys not only looks better to the hunter, but more "real" to the ducks and geese. An exception to this is in the early fall when many hunters intentionally smear their decoys with mud to make them more closely resemble the early-season ducks that haven't reached full plumage.

Decoys have been made of almost every conceivable material from corn shucks to aluminum, and in thousands of different styles. However, most of today's working decoys are made of either a hollow-hard plastic shell, plastic foam, granulated cork or wood. Each material requires a different bit of care and repair.

HARD PLASTIC SHELL

This is probably the most popular type of decoy today, and one of the longest-lasting. Shell decoys are usually molded in two separate halves, which are joined at the center line. These decoys also require the least amount of maintenance; a thorough cleaning after each season and occasionally regluing a crack or a parted seam is about all they require.

Because they're used in muddy and brackish water, decoys take on a coating of dirt and algae that can be a bit hard to remove, particularly if the decoys have been left in the water for the entire season. The best method of removing this algae and scum is to scrub the decoys with a solution made of a couple of gallons of water, a cup of household bleach and some laundry soap. Use a soft bristle brush to scrub off the caked dirt, then hose off the decoys and allow them to dry thoroughly before storing.

Inspect each decoy for cracks, paying special attention to the seams. If there is a crack or an opened seam, use a bit of plastic-model glue or household glue to fill in the void. The glued crack can be clamped with a long narrow piece of rubber cut from an old inner tube and wrapped several times around the decoy body. Pull the rubber clamp as tight as possible and tuck the end under to hold it in place. When the seam is dry, file down the plastic cement that has oozed out of the crack, being careful not to cut into the decoy. Run a thin bead of glue on the outside to completely seal off the crack and smooth it down with a piece of cardboard. If the crack is on the upper portion of the decoy, you should lightly sand the reglued seam to roughen up the shiny glue line.

Clean off the scum and algae that eventually collects on well-used decoys with a solution of water, a bit of household bleach to cut the algae, and laundry soap. Use a soft bristle brush or cloth to scrub the decoys, then rinse in fresh water and allow to dry.

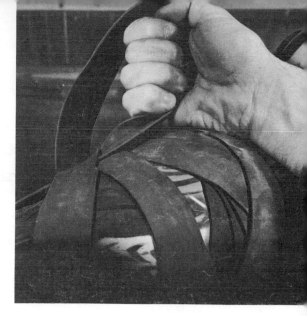

If a plastic shell decoy develops a crack, it's a simple matter to reglue it with household glue, clamping with bands of rubber cut from an old inner tube.

Some shell decoys have their colors baked in. However, most are "airbrush" painted. If any paint is worn off or chipped, touch it up with a decoy paint specifically formulated for fiberglass and plastic decoys.

PLASTIC FOAM

There are two kinds of plastic-foam decoys. One kind is an economical half-decoy made of expanded foam plastic. The foam cells are usually fairly large and the outer surface of the decoy is the same consistency of the inner foam. The entire decoy is extremely light, soft and fragile. Unless you are very careful, you'll be lucky to finish a season with these decoys. However, they are the most economical, and the lightest. So if you have to backpack into your favorite shooting hole, they may be your choice. A second kind of expanded foam plastic decoy is made of smaller foam cells and is more dense. The outer surface is quite a bit harder and quite durable. These decoys are naturally more expensive and just a bit heavier.

Repairing either of these decoys requires a few special techniques. The decoys should be cleaned with a solution of mild dish soap and water only, then rinsed or hosed clean and left to dry. Any brushing should be done lightly so you don't break loose any of the foam cells from the surface. You have also got to be careful to keep these decoys away from your outboard motor or gas tank, as gasoline will melt them.

185

Plastic foam decoys can be patched with plastic wood applied in thin layers in the gouge or dent. When it is hard, sand smooth.

The only glue that will hold properly on foam plastic is epoxy, so any broken heads or tails should be glued back in place with a two-part epoxy glue. Gouged spots or nicked holes can be patched with a mixture of epoxy glue and fine sawdust, or you can use plastic wood. If the gouge is deep, the patching material should be applied in thin layers, allowing each to dry. Otherwise, you'll end up with a sunken patch which may shrink away from the plastic. The patch is then lightly sanded down to match the rest of the surface and the patched area is touched up with paint.

One of the worst problems with some plastic foam decoys is the anchor cord screw-eye working loose in rough water. Coat screw-eye in epoxy and screw back in place.

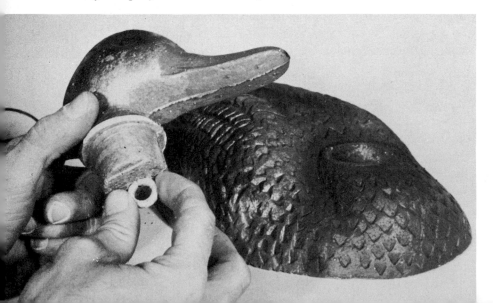

Because some paint and paint thinners will melt the plastic foam decoys, any paint used on these should be especially formulated for plastic. You can use a latex-based exterior paint as a substitute, although it generally won't wear quite as well. You can also use epoxy paints; however, these usually dry to a glossy finish. Ordinary baby powder can be added to the epoxy paints to cut some of the gloss.

One problem that frequently develops on the half-decoys is a loose anchor-cord screw. This screw-eye is usually turned into the bottom of the front of the decoy and easily works out of the fragile plastic, especially in a hard blow or rough water, as the decoy continually jerks on the anchor cord. To remedy this, smear the screw with epoxy glue and turn it back in place.

WOOD

Although there aren't many old-time wood decoys still working, a few dedicated waterfowlers are still using them. Because of the expense and time required in making and maintaining them, they're seen more often on the den shelf. However, if you prefer the realism of carefully detailed wood decoys floating in front of your blind, you will indeed learn to care for them.

The first chore after each season is to clean the decoys of any mud and scum. Again the best method is to use water, soap and household bleach. Rinse the decoys and allow them to dry thoroughly before the next step.

Go over each decoy carefully inspecting and noting any cracked or checking areas. If your decoys show signs of drying out, they should be soaked in hot, boiled linseed oil. Linseed oil should be heated in a double-boiler arrangement consisting of a couple of pans, never over an open flame. To properly flow into and seal the wood pores, the oil should be heated to a boiling stage. Using a soft bristle brush, scrub the hot linseed oil into the decoys and down into the pores. When the decoy surface is pretty well saturated, wipe the excess oil off with a soft cloth and place the decoy in a warm, well-ventilated spot to dry. It should be a temperature of 60 to 100 degrees.

Wooden decoys, new or old, should first be soaked in hot boiled linseed oil before painting. Old decoys should first be stripped with a good paint stripper.

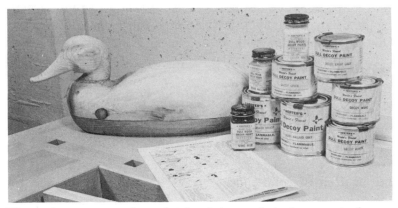

The easiest way to paint a batch of decoys is to buy a set of decoy paints for the particular species of duck you're copying. A chart included with the paints gives full details.

Paints used for decoys must dry to a non-glare finish.

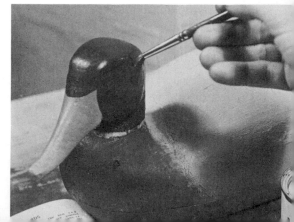

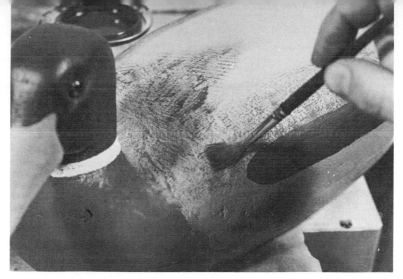

Dip brush in paint, then scrub off most of the paint to create a "dry-brush" effect for feathering.

After about an hour, examine the decoy for any sticky areas or spots where the linseed oil hasn't penetrated. Again wipe off any excess and allow the decoy to dry for a couple of weeks. If your decoys are pretty well battered with most of the paint gone, the old paint must be removed first using a good paint remover, then the decoys should be treated with oil before applying a coat of new paint.

Before applying paint to any decoys, plastic or wood, make sure they're perfectly dry. Do not paint outdoors or in cold or damp weather. Wooden decoys can be painted using decoy paint formulated for wood or with flat latex exterior house paints. One of the easiest ways to repaint your decoys is to use

Ordinary latex exterior house paint in the appropriate colors makes an excellent decoy paint. It can also be used as an economical base coat before applying decoy paints. This is especially helpful on granulated cork, which really soaks up paint.

189

Glass eyes from a taxidermist supply house adds realism to decoys. They are merely glued in a reamed hole, then the area is retouched with paint.

one of the decoy-painting kits from Herter's. These kits are made up to paint two dozen decoys of a particular species of duck and contain just the right amount of each color needed. Detailed painting instructions and a color chart illustrate where each color goes. Because of the pigments in some colors, they will dry somewhat shiny. To remedy this place all your freshly painted decoys outside in a safe, clean spot to weather for the summer. However, they shouldn't be placed where they will get too much direct sunlight.

Gouged spots or shot holes in wood decoys should be patched with wood putty, then filed and sanded down to match the existing surface. Broken heads, tails, etc., should be glued back in place using a two-part waterproof marine glue.

CORK

Original cork decoys are mighty scarce, but because of their long-lasting qualities and natural look in the water, there are still some about. Granulated sheet cork, a relatively new material in decoy making, promises to make cork decoys popular again, particularly with the amateur decoy carver.

The cork decoys don't require as much maintenance as the wooden decoys, but they must be "used" a bit differently. If left in the water for long periods of time, granulated cork decoys have a tendency to "waterlog" or take on water and gradually ride lower. Any water-soaked decoys should naturally be given the chance to dry out as thoroughly and as often as possible. Cork decoys must also be repainted or touched up after each season, much in the same manner as the wooden ones. However, the linseed oil waterproofing step is not required. The porous cork really soaks up the paint, so it's a good idea to "seal" the decoys with several coats of flat neutral-color latex exterior house paint. You can then follow this base coat with a final coat of paint in the pattern desired for the particular decoy. Cork decoys usually have wooden or waterproof pressed wood bottoms glued to them and a wooden head doweled into the cork. These should be repaired and patched in the same manner as the wooden decoys.

The wooden heads of cork-bodied decoys should be glued with a marine, resorcinol or epoxy glue.

PRESSED-PAPER FIELD DECOYS

At one time probably the most popular field decoys were made of composition pressed paper, but today these have practically all been replaced with plastic decoys. Of course, the main problem with decoys made of pressed paper is dampness. Store them in a cool, dry area with plenty of ventilation. Always allow them to dry thoroughly before sacking for storage. The outer surface of these decoys can be painted with flat latex paint for protection. A coating of clear epoxy finish brushed on their inner surfaces will help preserve them.

PROFILE FIELD DECOYS

Profile decoys are made of either pressed waterproof wood or quarter-inch marine plywood, and the best maintenance and the best protection for them is a coat of exterior latex paint. In storing them, stack them in a dry place. Don't stand them up or lean them against the wall, as they will warp and become hard to handle and set up.

RIGGING

Rigging lines should be carefully checked and tested after each season, replacing any that have become too badly deteriorated. Use only dark green line or one of a similar color. White rigging lines can flash an instant warning to cautious ducks. The technique of decoy rigging is indeed a highly personal matter, and debating a waterfowler's rigging method will not only get you a rousing argument but you probably won't be welcomed back. However, the main idea is to keep the cord and weights from tangling while storing and transporting the blocks. Several hunters I've hunted with like to use large swivel clips such as is used on fishing lines, clipping a rigged anchor to each decoy as they set them out. The rigging lines are then removed and stored separately when they take up their decoys. However, clipping and unclipping takes quite a bit of time and can be a pretty frustrating job when the temperature dips into the 20's, your fingers are numb, and huge white flakes are swirling in out of the Northwest. Probably the best known method, and my favorite, is to simply wind the cord around the decoy body, or better yet, around the keel if it is notched to receive it. A large rubber band cut from a bicycle inner tube will hold the cord and anchor in place. This is easily removed and stored in a hunting coat or boat while you're using the decoys.

Never use a light-colored line with your decoys. This photo reveals how visible it is, either in dark or clear water.

An easy method of transporting decoys by boat and storing them untangled as well is to place them in a sort of apron with pockets that will fasten to the sides of the boat. The decoys can quickly be removed from their individual pockets and set out from the boat. The apron is removed from the boat when you get back home and hung on nails in the back of the workshop or garage for easy, tangleproof storage of the blocks. The apron also works well for carrying decoys on your back, but of course the number of decoys is limited by the weight you can pack.

An easy and extremely effective way of carrying lightweight plastic decoys is in a plastic trash bag. If you're hiking back into some remote "duck pond" this technique just can't be beat.

Check the keels on your decoys. If you use your decoys in rough or open water, a well-designed keel is a must. Reglue any cracked or broken parts. Pay special attention to the hole in the keel through which the rigging cord is run. It must be smooth, with no rough edges to catch and wear on the rigging. Use fine sandpaper wrapped around a pencil or small dowel to smooth it down. If your decoys didn't ride quite right last season, perhaps they need balancing or the keels weighted a bit more. Using a bathtub full of water for a testing ground, attach tiny bits of lead to the keel or to one side or the other of the decoy to balance it out and make it ride properly.

ANCHORS

Anchors can be almost anything from a heavy fishing sinker to an old bolt. However, lead anchors usually work best because the steel anchors rust and cause rust streaks to form on stored decoys. Lost lead anchors can easily be replaced by molding new ones. A mold for large fishing sinkers, a melting ladle, a couple of bricks to rest the ladle on, a propane torch and a screwdriver are all that you'll need. The best anchors are from a mold for a 3- to 5-ounce pyramid shape weight such as used by surf fishermen. These will hold most decoys in place even in rough weather. However, if your decoys are extra large or used in extremely rough weather, you may need heavier anchors.

To make the anchors, chunks of lead are heated in the ladle until the lead turns molten. When the surface of the lead turns purple and scums over, it's ready to pour. Quickly scrape off any scum with the screwdriver and pour the molten metal into the mold. Allow the mold to cool and remove the new anchor.

One of the best anchors is made from a loop of aluminum clothesline wire and a lead anchor molded directly from the melting ladle. These mushroom anchors are easily slipped over the decoy head for ease in transporting and for keeping rigging lines untangled. To make these anchors, melt about a half a ladle of lead. Bend the clothesline in a loop with "ears" on the ends pointing in toward the center. Push the clothesline into the molten lead. When the lead hardens, pull out the clothesline-anchor.

Anchors can be stored on some decoys by merely winding line around the keel and holding it in place with a ½-inch-wide rubberband cut from a bicycle inner tube.

A more convenient way of storing decoys is to use a decoy sack with pockets for each decoy. The sack can be hung on the sides of a boat to keep the clutter out of the center of the boat. Hang it in the back of the garage during off-season.

Decoys without keels usually have the anchor cord tied to a small screw-eye near the front of the decoy. Recessing the screw-eye in a 1-inch hole will help keep the cord from snagging weeds or other anchor cords.

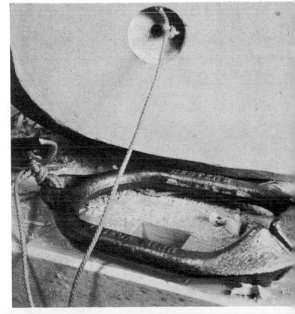

If the anchor cord is attached to a small hole in the front of a keel, make sure the hole is smooth and won't wear or chafe the anchor cord.

Anchors come in many sizes, varieties and weights including this commercially made model that slips over the decoy head for easy carrying and storing.

Homemade anchor can be made quite easily using a piece of aluminum clothesline wire and a hunk of melted lead.

You don't even need a mold. Merely place the lead chunks in a ladle, melt them, place the aluminum wire in place and allow the lead to harden. When cold, the entire anchor can be popped right out of the "mold."

BLINDS

Blinds for waterfowling can be anything from a simple pile of rocks or driftwood on a lonely beach to the most elaborate sunken concrete room, complete with heat and a telephone connection to a swank clubhouse. Repairing and maintaining them is just as varied. Of course, natural blinds won't require any maintenance; just pile on more rocks or reeds for the next season.

Cracks and seepage spots in sunken concrete blinds can be repaired by pumping out the water and patching the areas with epoxy water sealing compound or "Thoroseal," a quick-setting cement putty formulated for use in patching swimming pools and damp basements. This material can usually be applied even if a small amount of water is trickling into the blind. However, the patch must be applied in warm weather.

Sunken metal blinds don't usually require maintenance until they completely rust through. The best medicine for an old rusted metal blind is either to pull it out or use it as an outside mold, build an inner mold and pour a new concrete blind in this "shell." Make sure the concrete is anchored to the metal with screws, bolts protruding from the floor or walls, otherwise the shell may float when the blind floods.

This hunter has gotten a good start before the season, covering a metal river blind with tree limbs and grasses from the area. The blind will have plenty of time to "weather" before the season and will look quite natural.

Wooden blinds usually require the most maintenance, but they are the most popular and with good reason. As they can be built fairly portable, they can be moved seasonally if water or flight conditions warrant it. The most maintenance of wooden blinds consists of replacing rotting or broken boards. In replacing these, try to use boards of the same color and weathered effect. However, new boards can be stained with a coat of thinned paint to match any color effect. Newly built wooden blinds should be soaked in a waterproofing and repellent solution such as Penta. This should be done well before the season to allow the odors to leave the blind.

Portable blinds are another matter, and again these range from the extreme simple blind made of a roll of "chicken wire" onto which is tied marsh grass to an elaborate system of mirrors for field-goose shooting. Blinds using marsh grass should be renewed each year for the most natural-looking appearance. The grass should be laced or woven in place using "binder twine" or manila shipping twine.

CALLS

A good-quality, properly tuned call is a waterfowler's prized possession, and keeping them that way is a simple chore. Always carry your call in a pocket free from dirt, debris and tobacco. Keep it in its case when storing or not in use. A lanyard will keep it from being lost or dropped in the muddy blind floor.

If a foreign object lodges in the call, blow through it backward. If this doesn't remove the object, partially disassemble the call, gently raise the reed and try again. If all else fails, you may have to completely disassemble the call and clean it. Make sure you place the reed back in position exactly as you removed it. When you disassemble a call and remove the reed, you're apt to change the tone of the call, so it may take a bit of adjusting with the reed to get the call working properly again. Practice adjusting the reed, because knowing how to adjust a reed is a handy talent when weather changes abruptly or you've blown all morning on a call and its tone changes from the moisture.

If a foreign object becomes lodged in your call, it can often be removed by lifting the end of the reed and blowing backwards through call.

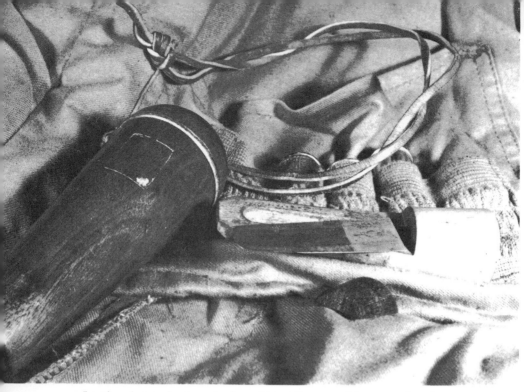

Leather lanyard prevents dropping call on muddy ground and knocking it out of tone.

If the finish on the call gets worn, renew it with light coats of boiled linseed oil applied with the palm of the hand and rubbed briskly into the wood. Do not use a varnish or spray-on finish.

If a call is accidentally dropped overboard, no harm's done. Simply pick the call up, blow through it backward for a minute or so, then reverse the call and blow on it naturally.

Linseed oil, rubbed in vigorously, will help to restore a battered finish on a call.

11 Archery Equipment

No one sport has benefited more from the technology and development of plastics than that of archery. By the same token, no other sporting arms are more steeped in the tradition and romance of yesteryear's hunting methods. Compare the 6- and 7-foot all-wood bows of just a few years ago with the short, sleek and fast-shooting wood-and-fiberglass laminated bows of today. A bow purchased today is a lifetime buy and requires no more upkeep and maintenance than a minimum amount of common sense. Unlike a gun, a bow can be slogged through mud and muck or left standing in a drizzling rain or wet snowstorm. It can be used in extremely cold weather and be ever ready to "fire" when that split-second opportunity presents itself. However, today's hunting bow represents a sizable investment and any outdoorsman will wish to prolong the life of the bow and keep it in top operating shape.

BOWS

Stringing the bow. There is actually only one major precaution needed for taking care of your bow, and it is important. String it up properly. Use either a stringing device or the step-through method and be careful to put equal strain on both limbs. In the step-through method, bring the heel of your foot off the ground to support the tip and keep it from digging into the ground. With your bow strung up, check to make sure the string is "seated squarely" in the string grooves, and that the bow limbs are not twisted. To check for limb twist, position the strung-up bow with one tip on the ground and with the string facing up. Holding the opposite tip, sight down the bowstring. The string should lie squarely down the middle of both limbs. If one of the limbs is twisted, it will show up, as it turns sideways under the string. Unstring the bow and carefully straighten the limb with your hands. Bend slowly a bit at a time, restringing and rechecking, until you have the string and bow lined up. If the "twisted limb" persists, check the string grooves; perhaps they are dirty, or the string has a lump or foreign object in it. This will cause the limb to twist off. If there is a great amount of twist and it cannot be corrected in this manner, take the bow back to your dealer. But do get it corrected, as a twisted limb will only get worse as you use the bow, and can become dangerous. When storing your bow at home, use a gun or bow rack to support it and keep it stored safely. For transporting by auto, use either a bow rack or a wooden case made to fit your bow.

The most important "maintenance" you can give your bow is to string it correctly. Place equal pressure on both limbs.

To check for limb twist, position bow with one tip on ground. Hold the opposite tip with string facing you and sight down string.

Protecting the finish. Although not required, it is a good idea to wipe down your bow after a wet and soggy day. One of the new "silicone" gun cloths makes an excellent cloth for wiping moisture off your bow. This prolongs the finish and keeps the wood from soaking up any excess moisture. All wood is subject to humidity changes and your bow is no exception. Unless the wood pores are completely filled with plastic or resin, as are some new "irridated woods" being used and tested in bow making, the wood is continually taking on and releasing moisture and adjusting to the atmosphere. So beware of extreme humidity changes. For instance, don't store your bow in a damp basement and take it out in the dry cold air for a three-day hunt and not expect some changes in it.

Finish on bow can be preserved with a good polish.

Although it is not so important, be careful of extremes in temperatures. If the bow has been subject to extremely high temperatures, allow it to cool slowly before stringing it. A day in the cold should not be followed by leaving it to stand by the fireside, only to pick it up in the morning, string it up and head back into the freezing weather.

Cleaning and repairing the bow. It's a good idea to occasionally stop and completely clean your bow. This not only keeps it looking nice, but gives you an opportunity to thoroughly examine it for any problems it might have developed. Dampen a sponge with soapy water and scrub off any caked-on dirt or dried mud. Do not scrape with a knife or any sharp object, as you run the chance of scratching the finish. When the bow is thoroughly clean, including the string grooves— which you may have to clean with a tooth brush or other small brush, wipe it down and dry it thoroughly with a soft cloth. If the bow is fairly new, apply a coat of good-quality, spray-on furniture polish, buffing with a soft absorbent cloth. However, if your bow is older and the finish is somewhat cracked and checked, use a good paste wax to "amalgamate" the finish and smooth it out. You can apply the furniture polish for a deeper sheen. Or, use a polish and cleaner especially formulated for bows. These are dual-purpose polishes and can be used to clean arrows as well and prevent them from picking up straw from target backs.

Some older model bows have leather "wrap-around" handles. These occasionally become loose around the edges, and can be reglued with ordinary household glue. If they become battered or torn, replace them with a winding of rawhide thongs. This provides a rougher surface for gripping in wet or cold weather and is easily applied. Again glue in place with household glue.

Although it is a rare occurrence, a laminated bow does occasionally separate. If you bought your bow new from a reputable dealer, you shouldn't have any problem. You can easily get it replaced. However, if it is a second-hand bow or purchased from someone other than a bow dealer, you may have problems. You can repair a delaminated bow at home. How careful you are and the extent of the delamination will determine your success in repairing it. Expensive tools are not required, only a little time and effort. If only the tip separates down for several inches, you should have no problem. If the entire limb delaminates, you may not get it successfully repaired.

If you decide to repair the bow, have several items ready before you start. You will need a good two-component, synthetic resin glue. One of the best, and used by most professional "bowyers" is Urac 185. This type of adhesive has a short shelf life of a couple of months, so have everything else ready when the adhesive arrives. You will also need a good vise to hold the bow while working on it, "waxed" paper, a couple of hardboard strips a bit longer than the bow limb and about a half-inch wide, and several 2-inch-wide rubber band clamps. These bands are cut from an old auto inner tube, starting in the center and cutting outward much in the same manner as you might peel an apple. (After you have used these for repairing your bow, stow them away. They're handy for clamping a dozen hard-to-clamp items.) You should also have some manner of applying heat to the bow while the glue is setting. If you are repairing the bow during warm weather, you can place the clamped bow in the back window of your car and leave it all day. However, in colder weather, you will have to build a heat box. This is a plywood box that the bow will fit into.

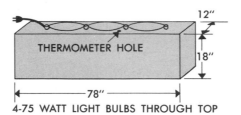

12"

THERMOMETER HOLE

18"

78"

4-75 WATT LIGHT BULBS THROUGH TOP

Heat box for gluing bow during cold weather.

It has ordinary light bulbs wired into the top, and a place for a candy thermometer for measuring the heat. Curing temperatures should run from 95 to 125 degrees for a period of not less than four hours. Unscrewing light bulbs regulates the temperature. I like to leave the bow in the heat box overnight at about 100 degrees.

With everything on hand and ready, mix the glue according to the manufacturer's instructions. Spread the laminations as far as possible, and using a brush, completely coat both surfaces as thoroughly as possible. Cover the handle with cloth to keep from marring it and place the handle in the vise. Place the waxed paper on the top and bottom of the bow, followed

Separated bow limb can be repaired using a special glue and "clamps" cut from an old inner tube.

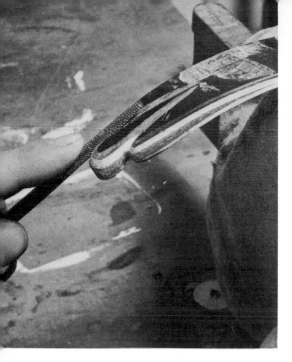

After glue has dried on re-glued limb, string grooves are filed clean, glue lines filed off sides of bow limb.

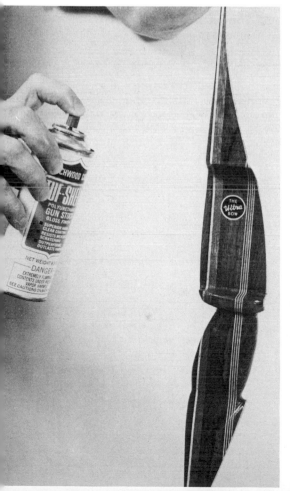

Repaired bow is given new finish. "Epoxy" or plastic gun-stock finish is best.

207

by the one-half-inch hardboard strips. Hold this assembly in place with a couple of C-clamps while you start wrapping the rubber clamps at the handle section. With one end of the rubber clamp secured beneath itself, start wrapping outward toward the tip. Pull the bands as tightly as you possibly can. If you have any bands left over, go back over again wrapping as tightly as possible. Place the clamped bow in either the heat box or a car window and leave as long as possible, or at least twelve hours. Check temperature about every hour or so until you're sure it will stay at a certain temperature.

After the required curing time, remove the rubber band clamps. Be careful of the bits of glue sticking to the bands; they can cut your hands like glass. Remove all the backing strips and waxed paper. The glue will have squeezed out of the sides of the bow and will have to be carefully filed off. The string grooves will also have to be cleaned out with a very tiny ⅛-inch round rattail file. When you have the bow back to it's original shape, carefully smooth the edges with fine sandpaper.

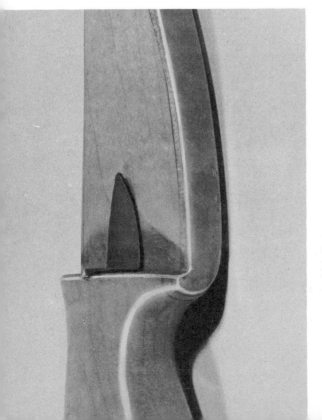

Missing or worn arrow rest should be replaced. A small piece of suede cut to fit bow window and glued in place with household glue makes a fine arrow rest.

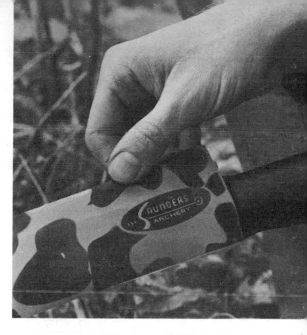

Bow can easily be camouflaged with tape made especially for this purpose.

Because of the differences in glue line, the bow will have to be "retillered." This is merely a matter of stringing it up, sighting down it to determine if either limb twists off to the side, and filing off a small amount of material from the side that is pulling the bow string off the center line. Again, make sure the string grooves are clear and of an equal depth. When you are sure the limb is straight, restring the bow and shoot a couple of dozen arrows, then recheck. With the bow in proper shooting shape, it should be sandpapered with extremely fine paper, and sprayed with a good gunstock finish.

If the arrow rest becomes loose or worn, replace it. You can use pieces of suede leather cut and fit into the bow "window," and glued in place with household glue. Or you can use one of the special "hunting" arrow rests that reduces noise. These small nylon brushes are fitted into a hole drilled a bit above the sight window shelf.

Miscellaneous. Some hunting archers like to fasten a tiny snip of bright string to the tip of their bows as a wind-direction indicator. Instead, I like to use a tiny piece of "duck down" glued to the very tip. The very slightest "breath" of air causes the feather to move.

Your bow can be camouflaged in several ways; you can use a bow sock, paint it or use camouflage tape. A dark crayon can be used to darken your string and camouflage it.

BOWSTRINGS

Each time you string up your bow, check the bowstring for any problems that may have developed with it. Wax it occasionally with a good string wax or a lump of beeswax. You can make your own bowstrings with a simple homemade jig, a "spool" of bow dacron and serving thread on a "bobbin." The modern bowstring is "endless," or made up of loops of dacron strung around the pegs on the jig. Follow the chart for the number of strands of V207 or 1100/2 bowstring dacron:

Up to 35#	10 strands
40 to 45#	12 strands
45 to 50#	14 strands
50 to 60#	16 strands
60 to 70#	18 strands
70 to 80#	20 strands

Bowstring should be waxed with string wax or beeswax.

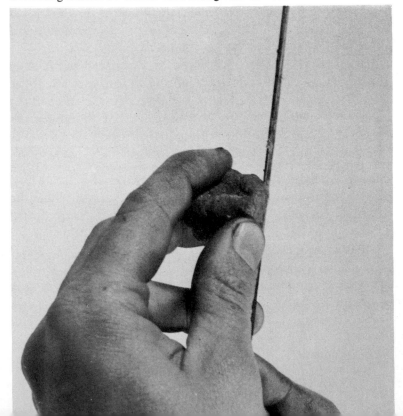

Never trust a bowstring that shows any amount of wear. Replace it immediately with a new one.

Making a bowstring.   To make a bowstring, position the pegs, or drive finishing nails in the board, the length of your old string. Tie one end of the dacron to one of the pegs and wrap the required number of strands. Cut off and tie onto the end tied to the peg. Pull the knot around about 2 inches and mark with a dark crayon about 1½ inches in from the peg on all strands. Pull the strands around until the marks are opposite each other in the center of the jig. Position one of the "loops" over the holding peg and wrap the other with serving thread. You can finish the wrapping with a rope whip serving. As you near the end of the winding, lay a loop of monofilament fishing line along the top of the bowstring. Tape it in place if you have to. Continue wrapping over the fishing line. After about seven to ten turns, place the end of the wrapping through the end of the loop. Pull the loop back through the winding, pulling the end of the winding back underneath itself. Clip off the loose end with nail clippers. When this is finished, pull the loops around until the opposite side is ready to be wrapped and wrap it with serving thread. With these two portions wrapped or "served," turn the loops until they fit over the pegs, with the ends offset about ¼ inch. Starting at the short end of the serving, wrap serving thread around the string sections, and continue wrapping for about 6 inches. This forms the loops on the bowstring. Measure about 5 inches on either side of the center of the bowstring and mark. Wrap this por-

211

tion and tie off as before. Apply a small amount of household cement to the ends of all wrappings. String up your bow with the new string and shoot a couple of dozen arrows with it. If you make the string a bit too long, it can be shortened to some degree by twisting it a few times. However, if it is too short, throw it away and make another.

Making your own bowstring is an easy and economical job, requires a homemade jig for holding string while you "wrap" it.

Homemade jig is simply a board with a nail or peg at each end, the same distance apart as the length of your old bowstring. Diagrams show how to tie and mark string material for wrapping.

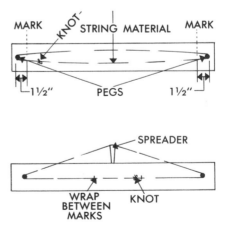

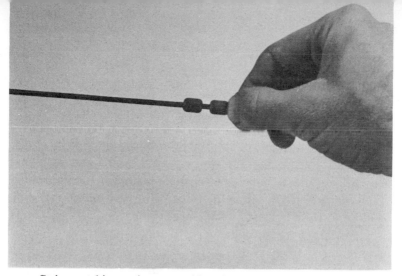

String nocking points can either be purchased, or thin strips of tape wound on the string.

For efficient hunting, you will want to place nocking points on the bowstring to position your arrow each time. These can either be purchased with small rubber "barrels" pushed in place or you can make them on the bowstring using narrow windings of black plastic electricians' tape. If you hunt in brushy country, you will want brush buttons to keep the tip of the bow from snagging on brush and undergrowth. These are slipped in place over the loops before stringing the bow. You can also add a string keeper. However, a large rubber band looped over the lower bow limb will hold the string in place as well.

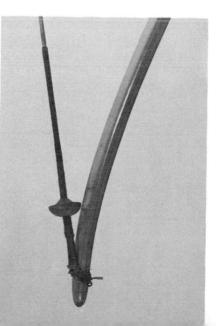

"Brush buttons" are a must for hunting brushy country. String holder is a large rubber band wrapped around bow and string.

ARROWS

Arrows are the expendable portion of your archery equipment, and considering the times they're used over and over are really quite a bargain. Some tips for lengthening their "life" are: when pulling arrows out of targets, grasp the shaft as close to the target as possible and pull straight out. A very effective target for broadheads is a block of Styrofoam pontoon material from your marine dealer. Always carry pliers afield for pulling arrows out of trees and stumps.

Upkeep of arrows.   Unless the shaft is broken, arrows are easily repaired. When nocks work loose, they can be glued back in position with a fast-drying plastic household glue. On three-vaned arrows, be sure the ridge on the nock is positioned in line with the colored feather. On arrows with four feathers, the nock ridge is placed between two of the feathers. Drilling a tiny hole in the end of the nock will let some of the excess glue squeeze out, helping to make a stronger fitting nock. However, make sure you wipe all glue out of the nock groove before it dries.

Loose arrowheads can be replaced in several ways. If they are field or target points, fill them with glue, place the point in position and use a hammer and nail to "dent" the edge and hold the point in place. Or you can use a dull "copper-pipe" cutter to "squeeze" the edge down on the shaft. For replacing broadheads, you will have to use the "nail-riveting technique." If you wish to place a broadhead on a shaft that has held a field point, use a taper-cutting tool or pocketknife to taper the end of the shaft down to fit the broadhead ferrule.

When pulling arrow from target. Never pry out using arrow as lever.

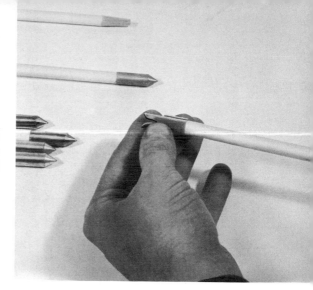

Nocks are glued in position with a household glue. Arrow shaft must first be tapered using a tapering tool.

Target points may be "knurled" on the shaft with a dull copper-tubing cutter used for plumbing. Or you can use a nail to indent a few spots around the edge.

Combination tapering tool cuts tapers for nocks as well as broadheads.

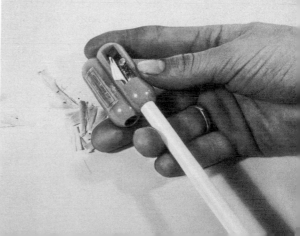

Sharpening arrowheads.   While we're on the subject of broadheads, every hunting archer should know how to get an extremely sharp edge on his arrows. An arrow is not effective unless the edge of the arrowhead is razor sharp and can slice through hide, muscle and gristle with ease. A dull arrow can only glance off, causing a lost shot, or a badly crippled animal. The edge of most broadheads have too blunt an angle when purchased, and to be really sharp, the edges should be thinned with a coarse bastard file. If the arrowhead is a two-blade head, you will not have much of a problem. Position the blade over a stump, or a block of wood and file away. However, if the arrowhead is the three-vane type, place it in a vise for sharpening. When the edge is properly thinned, use a coarse whetstone to smooth up the edge a bit. Allow the ferrule of the broadhead to ride on the stone to maintain the angle of the edge. Turn the whetstone over and repeat the operation on the smooth side, lubricating the stone with light machine oil. Always draw the blade toward the cutting edge as though you were going to shave the whetstone. Work on both sides to keep them equal. For an extremely fine edge, repeat the operation on a good razor hone or Arkansas stone, then strop the blade on a piece of leather such as the inside of your belt. If you take your time, you will have an edge as sharp as a razor and will be able to shave the hair off the back of your hand. For extremely effective broadheads, sharpen as above and add razor inserts in the sides. An arrowhead prepared in this way is the best assurance the sportsman can have that he won't lose game because of poor penetration and bleeding.

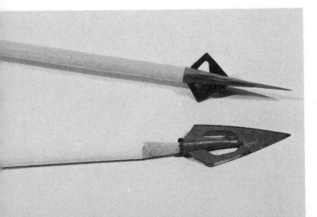

Broadheads are held in place with glue and by indenting with a small nail. Razor inserts add to effectiveness of broadhead.

Edge of factory broadhead should be reshaped using a coarse bastard file. Resulting edge should be thinner.

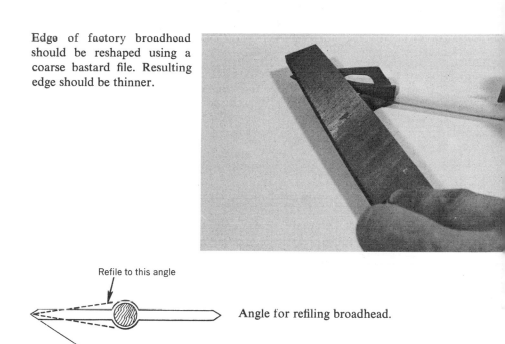

Refile to this angle

Angle for refiling broadhead.

Original angle

Keeping arrowheads sharp in the field requires carrying an arrowhead-sharpening device. This can be one of the V-shaped sharpeners that you pull the head through. These sharpeners put an extremely effective "hollow-ground" edge on your arrowheads. Or you can carry one of the extremely lightweight arrowhead files in your pack. Carrying a half-dozen freshly sharpened arrows in a leather quiver is about as fruitful as carrying a slingshot. By the time you get where you're going,

After reshaping and filing edge, it is carefully honed to razor sharpness.

217

For keeping broadheads razor sharp in field, use one of the "pull" sharpeners (*top*). It puts a "hollow-ground" edge on arrowhead. Or you may prefer one of the lightweight arrowhead files you can easily carry in a shirt pocket (*below*).

the arrows are completely dulled by rattling against each other and the leather. To keep your hunting arrows sharp, carry them in either a wooden back quiver or a bow quiver. If you use a bow quiver, get one that covers the tips of the arrowheads. When storing your arrows at home, remember an arrow is a lethal weapon and store it as such. Either place arrows in an archery rack out of reach of youngsters or keep them in a locked wooden box in a closet.

Upkeep of shafts.   Arrow shafts can be cleaned with a soft cloth, but should not have any wax applied to them. This only makes the shafts sticky and allows straw and debris to stick to them. Use only a good grade of arrow polish. Arrow shafts can be repainted by dipping down into a plugged pipe filled with thinned enamel, or into an "arrow-dipping" tank. The enamel should be thinned to about half with thinner and the arrows dipped at least three times. The arrow shafts are then lightly steel-wooled with fine steel wool, and the points, nocks and fletchings replaced.

You can replace a single fletching by applying a bit of household glue to the edge of the feather, then pinning the feather in place with straight pins. However, for a better job, use a fletching jig to hold the feather in position while it glues. It is almost a must to use a fletching jig when replacing all the fletchings on a shaft. For replacing fletchings, you may wish to use preshaped feathers available at sporting goods stores, or feather pieces, and use a feather trimmer after the feathers are glued in position. For just one or two fletchings each season, use the pretrimmed feathers. However, if you plan on redoing several arrows, use the feather pieces and trim them with a feather trimmer.

Arrow shafts may be repainted by dipping in thinned enamel. Dipping tank is long piece of electrical conduit pipe.

Shafts are "crested" using enamel and a small brush.

Fletchings are replaced using a fletching jog and household cement. For single fletchings use preshaped feathers.

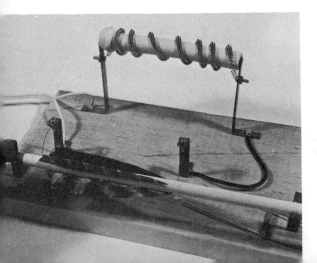

A fletching trimmer is necessary if you use untrimmed feathers.

Fletchings of hunting arrows should be given a good coating of waterproofing occasionally.

After repainting your arrow shafts, you may wish to "crest" them to identify your arrows from others. This is not as important to the hunting archer. In fact, my hunting arrows are a dull green with no cresting on them. Cresting can be done by hand by cradling the arrows in a couple of small blocks of wood mounted on a long wooden piece. The arrow is slowly turned by hand while you apply the crest or "ring" around the arrow with a small sign painters' or artists' lettering brush and thinned enamel. If you wish, you can "motorize" this operation using a small sign motor used in a store display. A rubber sleeve fitted over the shaft, then over the arrow nock, slowly turns the arrow while you hold the brush.

If you're going to be doing much hunting in damp weather, which is actually the most productive time for deer hunting, waterproof your fletchings with a coat of spray arrow waterproofing. It will help keep your arrows in good shootable shape.

MISCELLANEOUS

If you use a three-finger shooting glove, in time it will become hard and creased from use. Straighten the fingers as much as possible, work out the string creases and use a sharp knife or "wood rasp" to rough up the leather fingers and bring them back to normal. Check the elastic occasionally on your arm guard. It can be a bad mistake to let such a small matter as having an arm guard break on a deer-hunting trip and letting the sleeve of your hunting coat catch your string and pull your shot off.

Bow reel can extend your "hunting season." Always keep an eye
on the spots where it is fastened to your bow.

You can double your archery fun by going bow fishing for
rough fish. This is an exacting and yet brawling sport that provides the excitement of the stalk with the fun of battling a large
fish, but it can play havoc with your equipment. Because you
will be packing it through muck, mud and water, like many
archers use an old bow for this sport. Some bow fishing rigs
clamp onto your bow with a plastic-covered steel wire. Others
are taped on with electricians' tape. In either case, keep a sharp
eye on the spot where the unit is fastened to the bow. The
plastic-covered wires can become worn and gouge the bow
finish, while the black tape sometimes can really be hard to
get off if left in the hot sun for any length of time. Check the
reel edge to make sure there are no nicks or cuts to stop the
line from peeling off. Replace the line each year if you use
cotton line. If you use nylon, stretch it out and examine it for
any cuts or tears before the season starts.

12 Snowmobiles

If you own a snowmobile, you've got to know how to keep it running; it's as simple as that. When something goes wrong with your machine, you can bet you will be miles from a mechanic, service station or tow vehicle. Snowmobiles may seem complicated to the uninitiated, but they're actually designed for both ease of maintenance and dependability. The most important factor in keeping your machine dependable is a regular and proper "pretrip" maintenance. If your vehicle sees weekly action, set aside a bit of time each week for inspection and maintenance chores. You can alter this schedule to monthly if you use your snowmobile only occasionally, but you will have to be more careful with your inspections.

PRETRIP MAINTENANCE

As with all two-cycle engines, the single most important rule is the proper fuel mix. All two-cycle snowmobile engines do not use the same fuel-oil mixture ratio. Follow your owner's manual implicitly as to the proper ratio for your particular machine. If your fuel mixture contains too much oil, you will create excessive plug fouling; smoking and carbon will build up in the engine. If your fuel contains too little oil, you can seriously damage the engine; scoring cylinder walls, scorching pistons and rings.

Selecting the correct fuel.   The gasoline used should be a good grade of regular gasoline. Do not use a high-priced premium gasoline. The additives in premium gasoline only damage a two-cycle engine. The oil used should be for a two-cycle, air-cooled engine. This type of oil burns cleaner, is ashless and is thicker to provide more lubrication. Do not use an outboard motor oil unless it specifies for use with either water-cooled or

Fun vehicles that they are, snowmobiles can get you so far into the brush, so fast, it's almost unbelievable. It's imperative for anyone operating a snowmobile to know a little about repairing and maintaining them.

Regular maintenance schedule is the only way to keep your machine operating properly. Make it a habit to follow the same routine each time you inspect and maintain your machine.

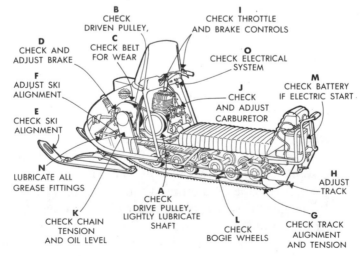

B
CHECK DRIVEN PULLEY,

I
CHECK THROTTLE AND BRAKE CONTROLS

D
CHECK AND ADJUST BRAKE

C
CHECK BELT FOR WEAR

O
CHECK ELECTRICAL SYSTEM

F
ADJUST SKI ALIGNMENT

J
CHECK AND ADJUST CARBURETOR

M
CHECK BATTERY IF ELECTRIC START

E
CHECK SKI ALIGNMENT

N
LUBRICATE ALL GREASE FITTINGS

H
ADJUST TRACK

K
CHECK CHAIN TENSION AND OIL LEVEL

A
CHECK DRIVE PULLEY, LIGHTLY LUBRICATE SHAFT

L
CHECK BOGIE WHEELS

G
CHECK TRACK ALIGNMENT AND TENSION

air-cooled engines. In a pinch you can use a quality automotive engine oil, SAE 30. But do not use a multiple viscosity oil. Always premix the fuel before pouring it into your snowmobile tank. In fact, it's a good idea to have two fuel cans. This way you can use one and always keep one filled, an easy way of keeping correctly mixed fuel on hand. Always use a funnel with a fine mesh screen to prevent water, dirt and debris from entering the fuel tank. The oil and fuel should be mixed at temperatures above freezing and the oil should be brought up to room temperature before mixing. Otherwise you will get poor "distribution" of oil in the fuel. When mixing, pour in a little gasoline, the oil required, and shake this portion vigorously. When this is thoroughly mixed, add the remaining gasoline. The fuel tank should be cleaned and flushed periodically to remove any foreign particles and water that may have gotten in. If the fuel in your snowmobile has been stored for some time, drain it off, flush the tank and fill with new fuel. Many carburetion problems are caused either by foreign particles in the gas or fuel line, etc., or by the gas vaporizing during storage, leaving gums and varnishes. These clog up the tiny vents and ports and may necessitate a complete carburetor overhaul.

Breaking in the engine. How you break in your machine has a lot to do with what maintenance problems you will have later. High performance two-cycles should be run in the higher r.p.m. range. They should, however, not be operated above ¾ throttle for any extended length of time, for at least the first ten operating hours. You can use full throttle in short bursts, but keep them spaced apart for the break-in period. By the same token, the engine should not be broken in at the lower end of its range or you will achieve nothing but plug fouling and carburetor problems. When your machine is new, the carburetor will be adjusted for a rich fuel mixture to assure adequate lubrication of the engine. After the break-in, readjust the carburetor to a somewhat leaner mixture, or return your snowmobile to your dealer for inspection. If you use your snowmobile at less than full throttle for extended periods of time, after break-in time, you will cause the plugs to oil foul. Changing to a different heat-range plug can alleviate some of this problem. Any time you start your snowmobile let it idle at least ten minutes before tearing away.

Checking the drive belt. Begin your monthly or weekly inspection and maintenance with the drive belt. NEVER RUN A SNOWMOBILE ENGINE WITHOUT A DRIVE BELT. Make sure the belt is in good shape, running smoothly in the pulleys. A worn belt causes a loss of speed as well as wear and tear on the pulley sheaves. If the pulleys do not work properly, the belt will hang up, turn sideways in the groove and burn off bits of rubber onto the sides of the pulleys. This all causes you to lose speed because it's difficult for the belt to then move out past the rubber burned onto the pulley sheaves. The belt should ride evenly in the bottom of the pulleys and move in and out easily. To remove a drive belt you can spread the sheaves of the pulleys by holding the fixed or stationary half of the driven pulley and rotating the movable half. This will

Properly operating drive belt is one of the most important factors in keeping your snow-mobile running. Belt should ride freely in and out of pulley sheaves.

Centerlines of pulleys should be positioned parallel to create the least amount of friction and wear on the drive belt.

allow the belt to loosen and slip off. (Be careful of mashed fingers.) An easier way that will work on some machines is to pull the belt deep into the clutch pulley. This allows the belt to become slack enough to slip off over the driving pulley.

Checking the clutch. The spring-loaded sheave of the centrifugal clutch should move in and out, although spring pressure should be fairly heavy. An easy check for the centrifugal clutch on the driven pulley is to twist the movable sheave a little and let it snap back. If it does not snap back, you should remove the clutch and check for a broken or weak spring or the lubricant on the shaft.

On some machines you can remove the clutch by holding the sheave and removing a nut on the cap. However, on most machines you will have to use a piston stop to hold the crankshaft while turning off the nut. This can be a purchased tool to fit your particular machine or a piece of nylon rope jammed down against the piston through the spark plug hole. Nylon works best, as the small bits of residue left in the cylinder when you remove the rope quickly burn away. Do not use a solid object such as a screwdriver or bolt. Turn the clutch wheel

Piece of nylon rope jammed down into cylinder after removing spark plug makes an efficient piston stop. Crankshaft is jammed, enabling you to remove clutch-pulley nut to get at clutch spring and shaft.

until it stops, then turn off the nut holding it. Lubricate the shaft with a small amount of "Hi-Temp" grease or petroleum jelly used quite sparingly. You may have to emery-cloth the shaft lightly if it has any rusted or badly corroded spots on it.

Using fine emery cloth and a bit of solvent, remove any bits of burned-on rubber from inside the pulley wheels and replace them on the shaft. You can remove the driven pulley by twisting to release spring pressure and removing the holding pin or governor, on most machines. Give the driven pulley the same treatment as the driving pulley, smoothing up any rough spots and removing any burned-on rubber bits. Replace the belt, jack the back of the machine off the ground and start the engine.

Do not stand directly in line with the clutch mechanism or the belt drive. On a correctly operating engine, the belt should not move while the engine is idling. On some machines it may creep a bit, but you can easily stop it with the brake. If the belt continues to run or creep, the machine may be idling too fast, the compression spring may be weak or broken, or the sheaves may still not be moving because of dirt or debris. Stop the engine and remedy the problem.

With outer clutch-pulley sheave off, inspect and repair or replace clutch spring. Inspect and lubricate shaft.

Also check the alignment of the pulleys. They should be in parallel alignment. This may take a bit of realignment. On most engines you can easily realign the engine drive pulley by loosening the nuts and sliding it into the position needed.

Checking the oil and chain tension. Remove the rubber grommet, or checking-port cover of the drive chain case, and check the oil level and the drive-chain tension with the end of your finger. In most machines, the tip of your finger should just touch the oil. However, check your operator's manual for your particular specifications. Also the oil in the chain case should be changed at least twice each season. This should be SAE 30-weight automotive oil.

In checking chain tension, refer to your owner's manual. However, a good rule of thumb is that the free play of the drive chain should be about ¼-inch in either direction. The drive chain should be checked after the first three hours of operation and thereafter for every twenty-five hours of operation or as required. If the chain requires adjustment, loosen the adjusting screws on the idler sprocket bracket and tighten or loosen the chain as required. Worn chain and sprockets can

Remove checking grommet on oil case of drive chain and check according to owner's manual. Refill with required oil. It's a good idea to drain each season and refill. Also check chain tension with tip of finger. Chain should have about ½-inch free play.

cause a lot of trouble, so keep an eye on both, and if either one becomes badly worn replace both.

In most machines, the drive chain is submerged in an oil-filled case. In others, the chain is lubricated with surplus oil from the crankcase. In this type there is usually a small oil line running to the chain. Check your machine for this and make sure it is operating properly. Some of the older models had "manual" oilers, and for these you may even need to occasionally remove the chain and soak it overnight in a pan of oil. A broken chain can be repaired using "connecting links." These are easily replaced with a pair of pliers.

Checking and adjusting the brakes. The brakes may be disc-type, wedge-type or shoe-type. In any case, the brake element is a friction device that rides against the side of the driven pulley. Adjusting it is a matter of varying the pressure on the pulley to give the best braking performance, yet not hinder the pulley's operation. A bit of trial and error is usually necessary to get just the right "feel." When checking the brake, check the full length of the cable for dirt, oil or any kinks, and don't forget areas where it is hidden by the "cowling."

Check and adjust brake. Snowmobile brakes are any one of three different friction types; drum, shoe or disk. In any case the braking element rides against the driving pulley and is adjusted to produce the friction needed there.

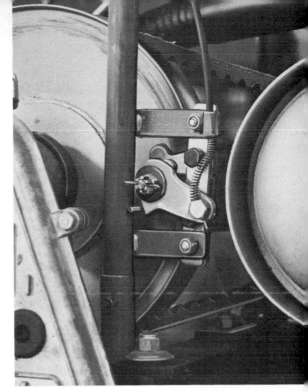

If track is running squarely machine will steer properly. If not, machine will have a tendency to run to one side or the other.

Adjusting track tension. Jack up the rear end of the machine until the track clears the ground and check the track for proper tension. Improper track tension results in undue wear to the track and drive components. A too-tight track causes wear, while a too-loose track is dangerous and can be thrown off. Tension must also be equalized on both sides of the track.

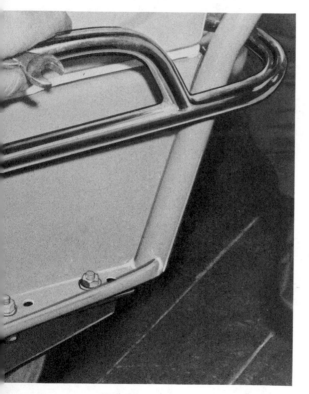

To adjust track, jack rear end of machine off ground, start engine, standing clear of track, and accelerate slowly. Adjust track so it rides squarely in center. Track tension should also be adjusted so you can just barely pass your hand between the bogie wheels and the track (without machine running).

If the tension is not equalized, the vehicle may tend to veer to the right or to the left even with the steering mechanism directed straight ahead. With proper track tension you should be able to just pass your hand between the bogie wheels and the track. However, this may vary somewhat, so check with your owner's manual for the exact track-tension specifications. The track tension is adjusted with the tension nuts located on the sides or back of the machine. With the vehicle still propped up and the track clear of everything, start the engine, and have someone slowly accelerate it slightly so the track turns slowly. The track should ride evenly, centered; if not, adjust it until it is well-centered and turns evenly on the rear sprockets.

A damaged belt can usually be spliced with metal repair lacing. In cutting across the track to apply the lacing, use a straightedge and carpenter's square to keep the cut at 90

New metal cleats can be attached to the rubber track with *"POP"* Rivetool and special rivets.

degrees to the edge of the track. Coat the edge of the cut track and also any tears or abrased areas of the track with liquid carpet binding, a form of liquid rubber available at most carpet stores. Always renew or replace damaged or lost track-drive inserts as soon as possible, as they can only lead to serious track damage. New cleats can quickly and easily be replaced with a pop rivet gun or even a cleat repair kit made especially for snowmobiles.

Skis should be aligned much the same as the front tires on your automobile. They should toe in about ¼ inch. Adjustment is usually a tie-rod system such as shown.

Checking skis.   For maximum steering control, skis should be aligned to have about a ¼-inch toe in. Aligning is an easy problem: place a yardstick at both front and back of skis and lengthen or shorten tie-rod connections for correct alignment. Line up the skis with the machine, loosen the steering connections, adjust the handlebars and retighten.

Miscellaneous checks.   Check the throttle controls and cable making sure everything is working freely.

Check and lubricate the bogie wheels being careful of the fittings in their thin aluminum hubs. Lubricate the entire machine with a grease gun, using an all-purpose winter chassis grease. Pump the gun only twice for each fitting.

If your machine is an electric start, check the battery and electrical system.

Lubricate the bogie wheels with Hi-Temp grease in their fittings. Be careful of the fittings in the thin aluminum hubs. They can pop out, requiring replacing the wheel.

Removing carbon buildup.   One of the problems with two-cycle engines is a buildup of carbon on the ports, caused by a rich-fuel/air mixture such as most snowmobiles run on. This leads to hard starting and poor engine performance. To remedy it, remove the muffler and exhaust pipe at least once a year to inspect. Any carbon buildup should be removed with a wooden orange stick or plastic scraper and a vacuum cleaner. While cleaning the ports, position the piston so the tiny carbon particles you scrape off won't fall into the crankcase. While the muffler is off is a good time to check the condition of the rings. They should appear shiny, and should spring back easily when probed with the wooden stick.

Inspecting spark plugs.   As mentioned in the chapters on "Chain Saws" and "Outboards," the spark plugs from your engine tell you how it is operating and what problems it may be developing. A normal plug will have a light gray or tan insulator tip. There will be very few combustion deposits and no erosion or burned electrodes. Burned electrodes on a plug mean: wrong-plug heat range, lean carburetor setting, engine overloading, an air leak in the fuel line from tank to pump, a loose carburetor mounting or clogged exhaust ports on a 2-cycle engine. A plug shorted out by combustion deposits means excessive carbon in the cylinder. In 4-cycle engines it means poor oil control; in 2-cycle engines improper fuel-oil mixture or clogged exhaust ports. If spark plugs have black tips, are damp with oil film, this means plug is too cold (heat range). In 4-cycle engines it could mean a worn oil-control ring, worn valve guides or overfilled crankcase. In a 2-cycle engine it means excessive oil or use of nonrecommended oil in fuel, idle speed is too low, idle adjustment is too rich, badly clogged air filter, a weak ignition output or excessive idling. Always check your instruction manual as to the gap setting of your machine. If it's hard to start in cold weather, set the electrode gap to the minimum recommended spacing. If the engine misses at high speeds, because of lack of voltage, the problem may be relieved by setting the plug gap slightly closer.

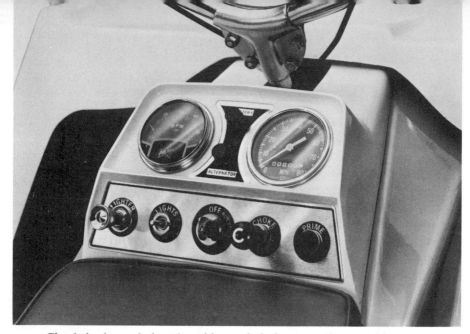

Check brake and throttle cables and dash connections, making sure there are no kinks or pinched spots in cables.

Adjusting carburetor settings. Although diaphragm-type carburetors are used on most snowmobiles, some have the float type. On a new machine, the carburetor has been tested and set for optimum performance during average or normal conditions. If your machine persists in excessive smoking or lack of power, it may indicate a need for a slight change in carburetor settings. Check your manual for the correct settings. Below are listed average settings, merely to get you started. After the engine is warmed up, you will have to refine the settings to get the machine operating properly.

The idle speed stop screw should be turned approximately two turns from the fully closed position. Give or take a half turn. The idle fuel needle should be turned one turn, plus or minus a quarter turn from its closed or seated position. The high-speed or main fuel-adjusting needle should be turned 1¼ turns counterclockwise from its fully closed position. You will probably find that your owner's manual suggests that the high-speed needle be adjusted ¼ to ¾ turns to the rich (counterclockwise) after the engine is warmed up, for final adjustment.

When making any carburetor adjustments, do so carefully so you will not damage needles and seats.

236

Always keep carburetor adjusted according to your owner's manual for the optimum in power and efficiency.

Cleaning the windshield. Using a special plexiglass cleaner made for boats, convertible windows or snowmobile windshields, clean the windshield thoroughly. This fine abrasive will cut out some of the finer scratches, making the windshield easier to see through. Or you can add a colored windshield with one of the new kits available. To merely clean a windshield, wipe it with a chamois, soft cloth or sponge dampened with Ivory soap. Follow with a dry, clean cloth.

Snowmobile windshields should be cleaned with mild soap such as Ivory, and a chamois. For removing scratches from the plexiglas use one of the kits on the market for renewing boat or snowmobile windshields.

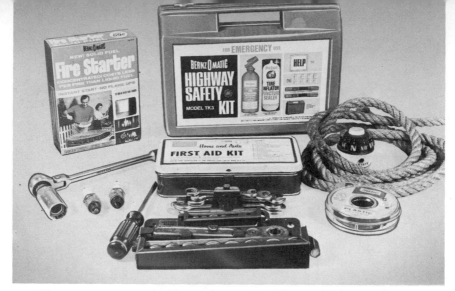

Always carry a repair kit on the snowmobile at all times. Kit should include tools, compass, rope, first-aid kit, fire starter, electrician's tape, spare spark plugs (properly gapped), spare drive belt, and a connecting link for the drive chain.

SUMMER STORAGE

How carefully you prepare your machine for summer storage in many cases will determine whether you've got a running or downed machine when the season starts next fall. Follow your owner's manual in reference to out-of-season storage. However, here are a few tips to get you started off to a roaring season next year.

Hosing down the machine.   Before you put your machine away, set it outside your garage or in some area close to a garden faucet and hose it down thoroughly. This is especially important in portions of the country where the machines are used on salted roads. The accumulated salt and water can eat through a machine in a year's time if not given proper attention. In any case, block the machine off the ground and hose it down thoroughly to get out all dirt, oil, debris and salt deposits. Use wooden paint paddles to knock and scrape off any stubborn spots of debris. If there are signs of rusting, scrape the areas down to the bare metal and spray thoroughly with a rust inhibiting, not resistant paint. While the machine is "drying out" use a good automobile polish to thoroughly clean and polish the cowling and metal portions of the machine. Use an upholstery cleaner to clean and brighten the upholstery.

Antirust measures.   To prevent the engine from rusting during the long storage period, you can use a can of engine-rust preventive. Follow instructions on the can for injecting it into the engine. Drive the machine into a permanent storage area, out of the weather, such as a garage, shed or lean-to and place it on blocks up off the ground. Make sure the vehicle is not resting on its track. Drain off the unused fuel from the fuel tank, remove the fuel line, fire up the engine and let it run the carburetor and fuel line dry. This is the one step not to forget. Fuel left over from the season before is thickened by vaporization and the left-over gums and varnish are pure murder for carburetors. Loosen the drive track and the drive-chain tension, to prevent the track from warping around the bogie wheels.

New spray lubricants are excellent for snowmobiles, can be used to protect clutches, springs and shafts from rust and corrosion. Lubricant can also be used to dry out wet ignitions in seconds as it displaces water.

Completely lubricate your machine according to your operator's manual, using a good grade of lubricant and 30-weight motor oil. Remove the spark plugs, place a few drops of SAE 20 motor oil in each cylinder and turn the engine over by hand. Replace the spark plugs, but leave the plug wire disconnected to prevent accidental starting.

If your fuel tank is removable, drain it, place about a quart of lacquer thinner and several pebbles in it and shake it thoroughly to break loose the gum and varnish that may have formed. Rinse it with gasoline and replace. Another thing you can do to prevent rust is to spray the inaccessible areas with a good rust-inhibiting spray.

When you take the machine out of storage for the season, you should relubricate all points, flush out the fuel tank, check the spark plug gap and readjust the track and drive-chain tension.

For peak performance and easy starting, use an oil specifically developed for the cold-weather operation of snowmobiles.

13 Chain Saws

One of the sportsman's newest "tools" is the lightweight chain saw. These practical little machines enable a camper to cut up enough firewood to last all night in a few minutes, or to clear a downed tree from a road or creek. They help the hunter to quickly build a deer or duck blind. According to one of the leading saw manufacturers, their lightweight model is becoming standard equipment in the tool box of many park rangers' pickups. However, their newest use is to cut holes in the ice for winter ice fishing. According to the engineers of most chain saw companies, this new "breed" of chain saw users has brought on a new kind of maintenance problem. When a professional saw operator uses a chain saw, he babies it. He has learned what to expect from it and how to take care of it. He may go so far as to even take the chain off the saw and soak it overnight in a pan of oil before using it the next day. Not so the new casual user; because he hasn't had the training or knows what to expect from the saw, he picks it up off the rack in the garage, goes out and saws a week's firewood or trims a few limbs and places the uncleaned saw back on the shelf until the next job. Another problem which has developed with the new user is sort of a vicious circle. He usually does not realize the importance of constantly using the chain oiler to keep the chain supplied with a generous amount of oil while the saw is operating. As a result the saw does its work less efficiently, and the user is dissatisfied.

However, with a regular maintenance schedule, today's sophisticated lightweight chain saw actually requires less upkeep than a gasoline-powered lawn mower. The most important maintenance rules to remember when operating a chain saw are to keep plenty of oil on the moving chain and to keep the chain tension properly adjusted.

Oiling chain-saw engines. Chain-saw engines are 2-cycle, and are lubricated by oil mixed with the gasoline. The correct mixture of fuel and oil is very important. Carefully follow the mixture ration specified in your operating manual. Use only a good grade of regular gasoline and a good-quality 2-cycle oil. Never use reclaimed or "used" oil. Mix the gas and oil in a container large enough to hold both the oil and gas amounts required and shake it after filling to thoroughly mix the oil and gas. Use a gas can with a flexible spout to fill the tank on the saw, and make sure the spout has a filter in the end. Wipe the fuel cap and the area around it before filling the fuel tank. The fuel tank should be emptied before storing the saw for any length of time.

Never start the chain saw in the same spot you've refueled it. Each time you refill the gas tank, refill the chain oiler. Use either a chain oil or SAE nonadditive motor oil at tempera-

When filling gasoline tank on saw, use a container with a spout and a filter to keep out dirt and foreign particles.

Each time you fill the gas tank, fill the chain oiler. Use a regular chain oil or a non-additive 30-weight motor oil.

tures above 40 degrees and an SAE nonadditive motor oil at lower temperatures. Wipe the area around the oil and fuel filler caps each time you fill them. Never operate your chain saw if the oiler is not operating. If the oiler is working properly, a fine mist or splatter of oil will be thrown from the chain when it is moving. One of the main problems with chain-saw operation is getting enough oil to the chain. Make sure you really pump the oiler, not just hold your finger down on it. Many chain saws have automatic oilers, but these are in addition to the manual oiler, and the manual oiler should be applied when the cutting conditions get rough. The automatic oiler should be adjusted as per your operating manual. A good sign of a poorly adjusted automatic oiler is oil seeping out of the saw while it is stored. Always check the oil level in the gear case of gear drive models and refill to manufacturer's specifications.

Adjusting chain tension. The second most important rule in efficient chain-saw operation is correct chain tension. A chain that is too loose is dangerous. A chain that is too tight will wear out fast, and also causes wear on the saw engine. A good indication that a chain is too tight is a "traveling" chain, or one that edges forward as the saw idles. (This can also be caused by the saw idling too fast.)

Make it a habit to check the chain tension the first thing when you pick up a chain saw. The tension is usually correct when the chain has a snug fit on the bar, but can still be pulled easily around the bar by hand. Be careful not to cut your hands on the chain; if in proper condition the chain can give you a nasty cut. A new chain will loosen after the first few hours of use, whereas a chain used for some time, or in some woods, may have a tendency to tighten and may need to be loosened every so often. To adjust the chain tension, loosen the nut on the bar-mounting bolt, hold the bar end up and either turn the tension-adjusting screw clockwise to tighten the chain or counterclockwise to loosen. When the tension is correct, re-tighten the nut on the bar-mounting chain. Recheck the tension before operating the saw. Never operate a chain saw at full speed for any sustained amount of time without actually cutting wood. However, the saw should always be operated at full throttle when it is under load in a cut. If the chain is properly sharpened and maintained you will not have to force the bar down into the cut, the chain will pull the bar through the log.

When the bar gets hung up or pinched by a log, use wedges to widen the saw kerf, allowing the bar to slip out. Don't try to force the saw.

Chain tension should be frequently checked in the field and adjusted as necessary.

When cutting, keep the bar off the ground and the chain will stay sharp longer. Don't force the machine, let its weight and power pull the chain through the wood.

Miscellaneous maintenance tips.   If a chain saw won't start:
1. Make sure ignition switch is on.
2. Turn choke lever to fully closed position (not required on a warm engine).
3. Check fuel tank.
4. Check for kinked or clogged fuel line.
5. If engine floods, turn choke to open position. To start a flooded engine, hold saw with muffler down and pull starter cord.
6. Remove spark plugs; if end is dark and damp, indicates carburetor needs adjustment. Turn the engine several times with starter rope to dry out crank case. Replace plug and start engine.
7. Carburetor out of adjustment. Adjust to initial settings as per owner's manual.
8. Check ignition system; remove plug, hold it about ⅛-inch away from engine housing, turn engine with starter rope, observe spark. If a good blue spark jumps across, continue looking for trouble in fuel system. If there is a weak or no spark, saw will require ignition maintenance.

Most chain-saw maintenance can be done by the sportsman with a few tools, however, some specialized repair work requires an expert chain-saw serviceman. The trouble is, the problem usually occurs miles from anywhere, and when you most need your equipment in good operating shape. A pre-seasonal checkup and regular maintenance will not only help prevent a "downed" machine back in the woods, but will familiarize you with your chain saw.

Cleaning chain saws.   Because of the very nature of their business, chain saws accumulate a lot of dirt, especially oil-soaked sawdust. It packs into the air filter, the openings in the fan housing, the cooling fins around the sprocket and the opening where the chain goes into the housing, or almost anywhere there is an opening in the saw housing. A heavy accumulation of the oil-soaked sawdust not only is dangerous but cuts down on the efficiency of the saw. So make it a point to stop after a couple of cutting jobs and thoroughly clean up the saw. Wipe

A clean air filter is vital to smooth running. Remove the cover, then the plastic filter. Soak the filter in solvent, allow it to dry thoroughly.

the housing down with a soft cloth. Use a blunt wooden scraper or an old toothbrush to scrape and remove the dirt and packed sawdust from all areas. You will have to remove a portion of the case to get at the sprocket and fins; however, don't neglect any portion you can possibly get at. With the saw thoroughly clean, tighten all screws and nuts and replace the housing clutch guard or whatever you may have removed. This is an excellent time to retighten loose nuts and screws and replace lost ones.

The air filter on the chain saw must be cleaned frequently. First, remove the cleaner cover, remove the air-filter screen, wash it thoroughly in gasoline (do this outdoors), then place it out in the open to dry completely. Keep the elements away from direct fire. It may take a bit of scrubbing to get the screen elements clean, particularly if it has been neglected for some time, but this is absolutely necessary. While you have the cover removed, wipe all sawdust and dirt away from the edges of the carburetor opening, being careful not to brush dirt into the carburetor. When the screen is dry, position it back in place and replace the holding cover. Do not operate the saw with the air filter or muffler removed.

Carefully wipe dirt and oil-soaked sawdust away from carburetor opening. Be careful not to drop particles into the opening.

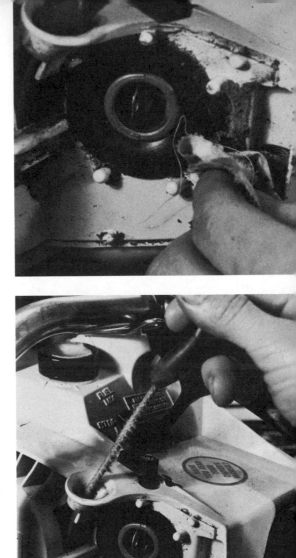

Slowly pull out starter rope and check for frayed and damaged areas.

With clutch, bar and sprocket cover removed, it is evident how much dirt and sawdust can get packed into a saw. This saw has been operated only eight hours.

Carefully clean out sprocket cover, making sure bar adjusting screw can work freely in its slot.

Muffler should occasionally be removed and the carbon deposits scraped from exhaust ports. Be careful not to drop carbon scrapings into cylinder.

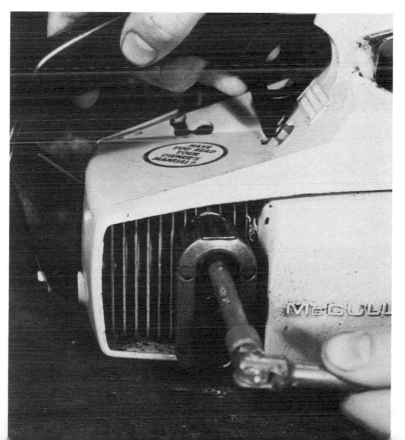

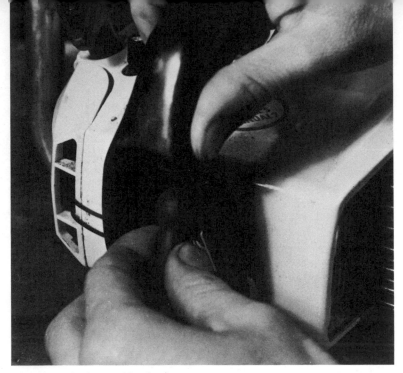
Check spark plug and lead wire.

Checking spark plugs.   Check the spark plug lead wire and insulator for any breaks or deterioration. Remove the spark plug with the proper plug wrench and carefully examine it. Examining a spark plug from an engine is much like a doctor taking a look at your throat; you can tell a lot about what or where a problem is just by the condition of the spark plug. Although many problems you may not be able to correct, you will at least have some idea of what is causing the problem when you take the saw to a repairman. A normal plug operating in the correct heat range for your particular saw should be a light gray or tan. There should be very little deposit on the electrodes and they should not be burned. A damp plug, or one with a wet-black carbon coating, indicates an overly rich carburetor setting. If the electrodes are badly eroded and there are several deposits of white or gray, or if the insulator is blistered, the carburetor setting is too lean, or the engine-cooling fins are blocked with sawdust or debris. If there is a lump of deposit extending from the center electrode to the outer shell, the cause is probably improper oil or incorrect oil-fuel mixture. If the plugs are in pretty good shape and fairly new, clean them with emery cloth or very fine sandpaper. Blow all the dust away and adjust the electrode gap to that specified in your operating manual. Wipe off all dirt from the porcelain insulator and reinstall the spark plug. If the spark plug is in bad shape, replace it with the proper plug as called for by your operating manual.

Checking the exhaust stack.   One item often forgotten is the exhaust stack. This should periodically be removed and cleaned of the carbon deposits that build up. Remove the stack and clean it by scraping away all of the heavier deposits, then wash it with solvent. Do not do any cleaning or scraping while the stack is in place on the engine, because of the danger of particles falling into the exhaust chamber.

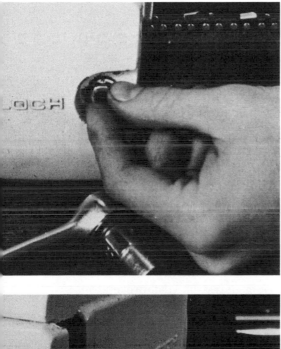

To adjust chain tension, loosen nut(s) on bar adjusting stud.

Holding end of bar up, adjust tension by turning adjusting screw. Retighten nut on adjusting stud when bar tension is correct.

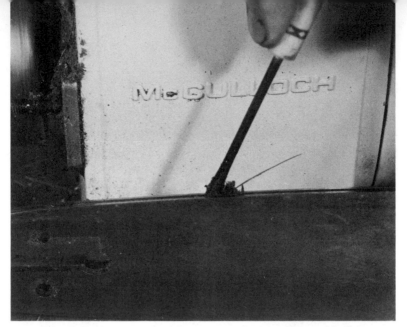

Slot in bar should occasionally be cleaned of sawdust and dirt. Use a small screwdriver or thin knife blade.

Remove the sprocket cover and brush the dirt and oil-packed sawdust from around the socket, the chain-entry holes, and in the sprocket cover. Pay particular attention to the chain-tension screw. This usually becomes quite packed, and if not cleaned can eventually effect the chain tension. Pull the bar away from the sprocket and examine it. The groove should be even all around the bar. If it is a bit pinched in a spot, gently force it with a thin screwdriver, being careful not to split the groove. If the groove is too wide, rap it lightly a couple of times with a hammer. If you've been cutting in wood that has a lot of pitch or sap, the bar will quite likely be covered with black gummy material. Using lacquer thinner and steel wool, remove the pitch. Brush all of the steel wool particles out of the chain groove in the bar, wipe the bar dry and give it a light coating of oil or a spray of rust prevention. While the bar is off, check to make sure it has no spots for possible future breaks. Replace the bar, position the chain on the sprocket and bar, and hold the end of the bar up with one hand. Replace the cover and nut and tighten hand tight. You will have to readjust the chain tension before completely re-tightening the nut. One of the problems encountered is to make sure that the chain-tension nipple fits into the slot in the bar so that adjusting the chain-tension screw moves the bar forward and backward.

Sharpening chain saws.   A chain saw is only as good as the cutting condition of its chain. Yet contrary to popular opinion, keeping a chain sharp and in good condition is not a mysterious hard-to-learn chore. Nor does it require very much equipment. Although the professional sharpeners use a chain vise, the chain can be sharpened right on the bar.

Position the saw with the bar in a vise, or if you're out in the timber, wedge the saw between a couple of logs or in the crotch of a log. Adjust the chain tension so the chain is a bit

To sharpen chain, fasten bar in vise, tighten chain snugly and file chain. Remove bar and chain, clean out the metal filings, replace bar and chain, readjusting the chain tension.

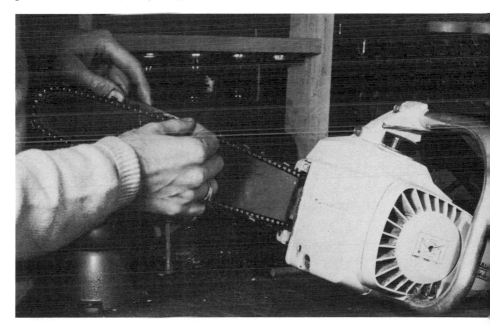

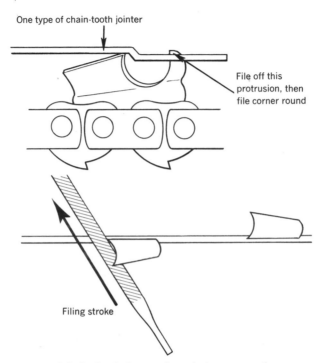

One type of chain-tooth jointer

File off this protrusion, then file corner round

Filing stroke

Method of sharpening chain-saw teeth.

tighter than usual, and where you can just barely pull it around the bar. If you're working inside a building, position a good light near the chain. Choose the correct "chain-saw" sharpening file to fit the size and type of cutter on your saw chain as determined by your owner's manual. Grasp the file on both ends and stroke the cutter lightly, pushing the file smoothly and evenly away from you. Do not allow the file to touch the chain on the backstroke. It's a good idea to turn the file occasionally to get an area that is free of cuttings. All the chain teeth or "cutters," as they're called, must be filed alike, so count the number of strokes and keep them the same height. You can check the height of the cutters by laying a small flat file along the top of the cutters. File the cutters going one direction, turn the saw around to file the opposite cutters.

If you're doing a touch-up job only, go no further. However, if you're "refurbishing" a pretty badly beat-up or dull chain, you will also have to file the depth gauges down according to the amount you've filed the cutters. (The depth gauge of the chain cutter determines the size of the chip that the tooth removes.) You will have to purchase a small hand tool called a jointer for this job. The jointer is positioned over the chain, the gauges are shown in a slot enabling you to file them flush with the "jointer" surface. You should also make a careful examination of the "tangs" or under side of the cutters and file any sides that are burred or nicked.

If you have sharpened the entire chain, it's a good idea to remove the chain and bar when you've finished sharpening and completely clean the bar and chain to keep from throwing the tiny metal cuttings back into the sprocket and clutch.

Repairing chain saws. If a chain breaks, and you have connecting links handy, it can be easily repaired. The rivets in the broken links are removed using a small steel punch and a heavy strap of steel with a hole in it. The connecting link, or links, is replaced using the rivets provided. Use light tapping blows to set the rivet heads and to keep from smashing

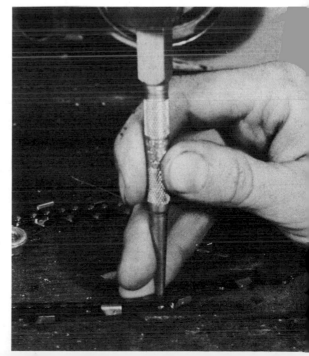

To repair a broken chain, punch out the rivets in broken link with a metal punch and scrap piece of metal with hole in it. Replace the broken links with connecting links, riveting with the metal punch.

the joint or breaking the rivet. With the new links in place, file them to match the surrounding links. When replacing the links make sure that the countersunk portion of the hole is to the outside.

Daily maintenance.   Chains should frequently be cleaned with a stiff bristle brush and light oil. After each day's use, check the chain for wood chips, or tight joints that might cause breakage.

If you use your chain saw for cutting ice-fishing holes, as a lot of fishermen do, remove the chain after the day's work and allow it to soak overnight in a pan of oil. Or you can spray it thoroughly with rust-penetrating oil, turning it around the bar several times to work the oil into the sprocket.

If you use your saw for cutting holes in ice, be sure and wipe down the bar and chain afterwards. Spray with a light coat of penetrating rust-inhibiting oil.

14 The Warbag

In earlier days, the warbag was a small pouch used by the Plains Indians to carry the various war-medicine articles needed to protect the warrior and give him help against his enemies. Today the term means almost any small pouch that is used to carry personal items. It is carried by Western horsemen and foot travelers alike. Some items may be carried in various pockets by outdoorsmen and the list changes from person to person like the old adage, "one man's prize, another's junk." But in any case, a pack-packer or canoe camper will prize a good warbag and use it to carry: a pocketknife—one with an awl, a can opener and at least two good blades that will stay sharp. The warbag should also contain a well-maintained first-aid kit and a snake-bite kit. It should also have a good compass and topographic and other maps of the area you're in, waterproof matches, a candle, and most of all a repair kit. It should contain a small sewing kit, insect repellent, sun lotion, sunburn lotion and, of course, your own personal-care items.

Auto campers can have a "warbag" too. In fact, mine never comes out of the back of my station wagon. My auto warbag is really a wooden box that will fit in the back of the car without taking up too much room. It is used to hold a various assortment of items that might be lost under the seat or shuffled around with the larger items. I constantly change the contents of the box to fit the seasons as I run through the fishing season into duck-hunting season, deer and quail hunting, then back to fishing again. I always carry a full suit of clothes, including underwear, strapped to the top lid of the box, and a heavy wool sweater, extra rain wear and a windbreaker.

More than once I've been dunked on an outdoor outing and blessed myself when I got back to my car and pulled on dry

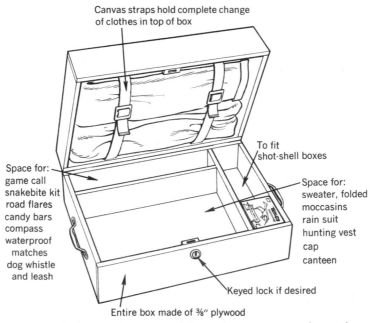

Canvas straps hold complete change
of clothes in top of box

To fit
shot-shell boxes

Space for:
game call
snakebite kit
road flares
candy bars
compass
waterproof
matches
dog whistle
and leash

Space for:
sweater, folded
moccasins
rain suit
hunting vest
cap
canteen

Keyed lock if desired

Entire box made of ⅜" plywood

Homemade box packs personal items in auto on outdoor trips.

clothes. The idea started a couple of years ago when I was
duck hunting. My blind was several miles up an old river
slough, and as I walked back to the blind I had to wade a
couple of knee-high creeks. I sat in the blind all morning and
the weather changed from bad to worse. It started raining,
changed to snow, then to sleet, and the ducks were pitching in
like hail. Naturally, I didn't want to leave. About noon I filled
out my limit and started to walk the several miles back to my
car. When I came to the first creek it was quite a bit fuller than
before; however I made it without mishap. When I came to the
second, it was pouring over the bank and really roaring. Needless to say, when I got back to my car, with my clothes frozen
stiff as boards and my feet numb, I would have given almost
anything for a warm suit of clothes. However, I had about
seventy miles to drive home, and it took most of it to warm up.

My auto warbag also has a heavy-duty rain parka in a camouflage pattern, a pair of lightweight folding camp-moccasins, a first-aid kit, snake-bite kit, road-flare kit, emergency-food kit made up of several candy bars sealed in a couple of plastic bags, a compass and waterproof matches encased in a small container. I also carry a couple of sheath knives, a small-game hoist, small backpack and short axe.

One section of the box is divided to fit shell boxes, and I keep shells to fit the changing hunting season. Also during duck season I keep a couple of duck and goose calls, and also a squirrel call, predator call, a couple of boxes of .22-rifle shells, and a lightweight shell vest. If I go duck hunting and the ducks aren't flying, all I've got to do is break out the quail loads, or perhaps the squirrels are gathering nuts in the pin-oaks surrounding the duck-hunting grounds. Which brings up another trick I have for turning an otherwise sour hunting or fishing day into a fun and fruitful day. I also carry a box of plastic bags. Now maybe the doves aren't cooperating, so I'll just go down by the river bank where I earlier saw a vine of wild grapes and pick enough for a batch of jelly. Or maybe after hiking back into a small lake for bass I find it's covered with moss and unfishable. If I've got a few plastic bags, it might be blackberries, or even mushrooms.

WATERPROOF MATCHES

Even though you keep a few in your warbag, every outdoorsman should carry a container of waterproof matches on his person. Even if you're only going out for an hour or so crappie fishing on a sheltered lake, or perhaps rabbit hunting a mile or so from home, accidents can happen and a good fire not only can provide warmth and comfort, but act as a signal if need be.

There are several ways you can assure you'll always have a few waterproofed matches with you. Some sportsmen like to drill a small hole in their gunstocks, place a few matches in the hole and tap a tapered wooden plug back in the hole. If you need matches, dig out the plug with a sharp knife. If you use this method, it's also a good idea to put in a couple of small candles. Because candles burn longer, they're easier to

Matches can be waterproofed by dipping them individually in melted paraffin, then standing them in a chunk of foam plastic to harden.

start a fire with. I also like to keep waterproof matches in my tackle box. On more than one occasion I've had to sit out a storm on a cold, lonely beach, where a roaring fire made everything seem almost comfortable.

You can buy waterproofed matches sealed in waterproof containers, but you can also make your own quite easily. Dip the heads of several large wooden kitchen matches (strike-anywhere) in melted paraffin. Dip each match individually, then stand it in a chunk of Styrofoam to cool and harden. While they're cooling, make a waterproof container using a spent 16-gauge and 20-gauge shotgun shell. Using a sharp razor, trim off the torn and ragged ends of the shells. Place the cooled and waterproofed matches in the 20-gauge shell, slide the 16 over the 20 and coat the joint and both shells liberally with melted paraffin. While you're at it, it's not a bad idea to make several of these sets and place them in strategic spots.

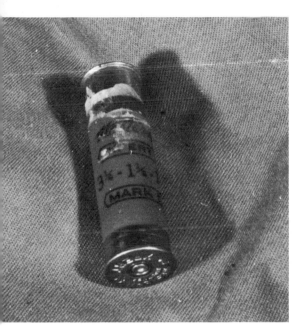

Waterproof match case can be made from 16- and 20-gauge shells. The shell cases are trimmed, the matches dropped inside, then the 16 slipped over the 20 and covered with a thin coating of paraffin.

COMPASS

There isn't much that can go wrong with a good compass. It either works, or it doesn't. However, at least once each season check your compass so you know if it is working properly. You should also check the contents of your first-aid kits, both those kept in your auto and smaller personal kits. Replace any items that may have been used or those that may be outdated. This is also a good time to examine your snake-bite kit, making sure it's ready for use. If you carry an antivenom kit, make sure it's not outdated.

SURVIVAL KITS

One item all outdoorsmen should carry at all times afield is a tiny survival kit. It has to be so small that you hardly notice it, and in fact make a habit of keeping it in your pocket. I carry one that is so small I can easily keep it with me at all times, even when I'm flying cross country. Yet it has the essentials for basic survival in almost all areas, except for extreme desert or arctic conditions.

It contains one needle and a couple yards of thread, about 10 feet of fine copper wire for snares, 15 feet of 6-pound test monofilament fishing line wrapped around two waterproofed wooden matches, a half-dozen small hooks and two split shot. There is also one single-edge razor blade and one Band-Aid. This is all fitted into a tiny plastic box that fishing tackle such as split shot is purchased in. The whole unit is light and compact enough that you hardly even know you're carrying it. To be on the safe side, I again store one in several spots—one in my backpack, one in my auto glove box and one in my bird-hunting vest.

Sections of maps will last longer if coated with varnish. Place the cut-out map section on waxed paper and coat the top side with varnish. Allow to dry, then turn over and coat the other side.

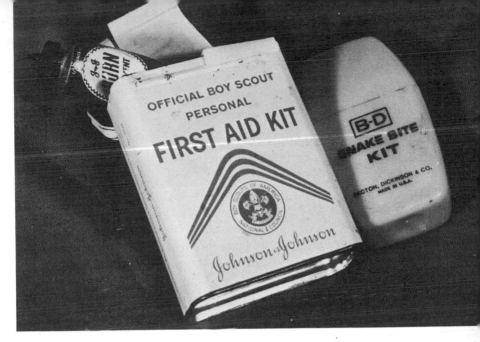

Every outdoorsman should carry at least a small first-aid kit on any trek into the woods. It should be checked regularly and kept replenished. If you're headed into snake country, make sure you have a good snakebite kit as well.

Another item that many outdoorsmen wouldn't be without is a tiny but sufficient survival kit. Kit shown is small enough to go almost unnoticed in pocket, yet provides essentials for survival.

FLASHLIGHTS AND LANTERNS

A good bright light is a must for any fisherman or hunter who ventures out after nighttime. This point was well made to me during a recent duck season. I had drawn a blind in a public shooting preserve several miles away from the nearest boat ramp, so I had to cross the lake in the early-morning pitch black. The crossing was complicated by the fact that the lake was not only shallow but stumped filled. To my dismay, when I got the boat loaded, launched and started out, my "one and only" boat lantern was so dim I could barely make out a stump with it a few feet away. I cautiously progressed across the lake and finally found my blind, but by the time I had, it was almost too late to set out my decoys for the first morning flight. Before my next trip I had a properly working lantern with fresh batteries, plus an extra stored under the boat seat.

Frequently check your lantern or flashlight so you won't have trouble in the field. However, when trouble develops it is usually in one of three areas. If the unit won't work at all, check the bulb and batteries on a sporting-store tester, or by

Corrosion is the problem with any flashlight or lantern. Occasionally disassemble lantern or flashlight and scrape and clean corrosion from interior of case, connections, etc.

wiring across with a small piece of wire, taping one piece to the threads of the bulb and touching the end of one to the bulb tip. If the bulb works, clean all the contact points inside the flashlight or lantern with fine emery paper, or scrape them clean with a pocketknife. One of the best tools for cleaning contacts is the "pencil"-type typewriter eraser. Stretch the spring in the base of small flashlights a bit and clean the spring end. Clean the switch, making sure the contact strip of the switch can touch the batteries. In a lantern, make sure all the contact strips are properly cleaned, and touch the battery terminals. You may note a bit of rust in the bottom of the flashlight caps. This is one of the most common problems with metal flashlights. Clean the rust out, then spray the area with a rust-penetrating oil.

Index